GW00730686

Alexa

Complete User Guide for
Your Amazon Echo
Device.

2021

SATISFACTION
★ ★ ★
100%
MONEY BACK
★ ★ ★
GUARANTEED

100+1
Things to
Ask Your
Personal
Assistant

Alexa:

2021 Complete User Guide for Your Amazon Echo Device. 100+1 Things to Ask Your Personal Assistant

ALEXA

ISBN: 9798509351648

CONTENTS

Description

Alexa is a virtual personal assistant designed to compete for Apple Siri, Google Now, and others. Alexa, who has constructed Amazon's secret Lab 126, can hear voice commands and respond to the necessary responses to your task. Alexa can let you listen to Spotify music, make to-do lists, shop, or even manage your smart home gadgets such as Google's Thermostat or Philips Hue.

Amazon Alexa opens a whole new world full of possibilities. From taking control of your home appliance to keeping you busy on the road.

The idea of connecting intelligent speakers to the voice-controlled exceptional personal assistant service Alexa can respond to changeable names such as Computer, Echo, or executing several pre-set functions like the current weather, build lists, timers, etc. This book is a guide to take you through procedures of gaining a fundamental understanding of the virtual assistant developed by Amazon. Our book gives a thorough explanation of several devices with the virtual assistant mechanism and how to set your device with it. Its several enhancement skills and wonderful commands you can pass to the service. The book provides lots of insight into utilizing IFTTT, tricks for streaming music and apps, tips for echo devices, and different usage tips that can make your echo devices better. It also discusses various productive and troubleshooting tips.

This book is packed full of information to increase your practical understanding. This book consists of the general comprehension of the virtual assistant mechanism, its enhancement skills, etc.

Discover Alexa in full effect and learn amazing tips that help you manage your device better. From setting up your Alexa device to guiding you on how to choose the right skill for your Echo device. Do you have a capital one account? Discover how to access your account balance and request for a loan.

Whether on Echo dot, Echo Auto, or Echo show, our step by step guide works on all Alexa compatible devices.

Introduction

What is Alexa?

In 2011, Amazon introduced the first Echo, a voice-activated speaker. As of September 2017, there were now about 10,000 Echo products on the market. The devices work much like smartphones and smartwatches do, providing one-touch access to an ever-growing array of Amazon services.

Alexa is a virtual assistant that responds to verbal commands, such as asking it to play the song "Somewhere over the Rainbow." The devices are powered by artificial intelligence technology that, as of 2017, could interpret the user's voice as "Alexa" with the correct answer to any question, like saying, "Alexa, what's the capital of Latvia?"

What does Alexa do?

In the past year, Alexa has gotten a series of new features and capabilities, including:

Subtitles on supported Prime video content. Most people have access to Amazon Prime, the company's membership program. For people without Prime, the device allows you to watch movies and television shows with closed captions or voice-dubbing, and sometimes even with subtitles.

Most people have access to Amazon Prime, the company's membership program. For people without Prime, the device allows you to watch movies and television shows with closed captions or voice-dubbing, and sometimes even with subtitles. Alex-and-Apple mashup. Until recently, if you wanted to play music, watch a movie, or even read a book to your child, you had to have Apple's HomeKit setup. Now, you can have Alexa interact with your Apple devices, such as the Apple HomePod smart speaker. The integration enables people to ask Alexa to play music on their Apple device or check the weather on their Apple devices by simply saying, "Alexa, ask Apple HomeKit to play Bob Dylan."

Until recently, if you wanted to play music, watch a movie, or even read a book to your child, you had to have Apple's HomeKit setup. Now, you can have Alexa interact with your Apple devices, such as the Apple HomePod smart speaker. The integration enables people to ask Alexa to play music on their Apple device or check the weather on their Apple devices by simply saying, "Alexa, ask Apple HomeKit to play Bob Dylan." Adaptive audio. Users can now customize Alexa's responses to different users by setting a "wake word" for each user. Alexa hears each user's "wake word" only once.

Users can now customize Alexa's responses to different users by setting a "wake word" for each user. Alexa hears each user's "wake word" only once. Smart home improvements. As of September, Amazon has expanded the number of Alexa-compatible smart home products from about 6,000 to more than 15,000. Alexa can now control smart locks, thermostats, smoke detectors, and even light bulbs, Amazon says.

Amazon has expanded the number of Alexa-compatible smart home products from about 6,000 to more than 15,000. Alexa can now control smart locks, thermostats, smoke detectors, and even light bulbs, Amazon says.

Worldwide launch of audiobooks. Amazon is now offering Audible audiobooks, which were previously only available in the U.S. The offerings include popular titles, like "The Woman in the Window," "Unbroken," and "Becoming Steve Jobs."

Amazon is now offering Audible audiobooks, which were previously only available in the U.S. The offerings include popular titles, like "The Woman in the Window," "Unbroken," and "Becoming Steve Jobs." Voice calling. Starting in late September, Amazon added voice calling to its Alexa app. You can now make phone calls to the U.S. and Canada from anywhere in the U.S. or Canada, through the Alexa app. You can also make and receive international calls, including to more than 200 countries and territories.

Starting in late September, Amazon added voice calling to its Alexa app. You can now make phone calls to the U.S. and Canada from anywhere in the U.S. or Canada, through the Alexa app. You can also make and receive international calls, including to more than 200 countries and territories. Alexa falls for its own joke. Alexa once tricked Alexa into playing its own jokes. One of the jokes was to ask Alexa to, "Call my mother." While it was typical of jokes Alexa has played in the past, this one worked. A user asked Alexa to call her mother and the virtual assistant obliged, claiming that her mother was currently unconscious. Alexa's laugh added an extra punch.

What role of Alexa voice helper in every day?

While the list of uses is increasing day by day, the most common use of this smart assistant is the asking of the weather, news, and other general information. Many services provide weather forecasts in real time. For example, BBC weather will let you know the weather details in seconds while Wunderlist will not only tell you the weather but also add a to-do-list to your shopping list.

Other common use cases are asking about the traffic, planning a trip to a place, ordering things from Amazon stores, accessing music or other audio libraries, and playing jokes on friends.

But it is not only through Amazon that you can use Alexa. Some developers have made their voice recognition APIs available for different platforms such as Facebook, IFTTT,

Mozilla, iOS, Google Home, iOS, and Android, allowing the users to connect it to their favorite apps.

Moreover, the developers can build more advanced voice interaction through other APIs like Google's IFTTT and Apple's SiriKit. While these apps are more focused on implementing the smart home appliances, developers have also built intelligent assistants in the form of messenger bots. For example, WhatsApp already has an Alexa app. You can now use the app to ask Alexa to tell you how your day has been. However, the integration with WhatsApp's native app is not supported yet.

How to set up Amazon Echo or Alexa?

Setting up an Alexa-powered speaker is pretty easy. The process is the same as installing an app on your smartphone.

First, go to the Alexa App and enable your new Alexa-powered speaker. To do this, go to the "Settings" tab and then select "Manage Your Skills" from the "Skills" sub-menu. Here, you can add the new Alexa-powered speaker and start using it immediately. After enabling the new skill, the Alexa-powered speaker will appear under "My Skills" list.

Once you are done setting up the device, you can go to Amazon's Alexa app and link your Amazon account to the Alexa speaker. You need to enter your login credentials and password if you are not already an Amazon Prime member.

Next, search for the skill you want to use with Alexa. For example, if you want to listen to a radio station, simply type "Radio" in the search bar and you will find all of the radio stations available on the Alexa-powered speaker. The skill will show up on the menu and you can activate it. Then you can use Alexa to play the radio station or add it to the "My Skill" list. If you want to play a song from an artist, just ask Alexa to play the song by the artist's name. For example, ask Alexa to play Taylor Swift songs or lyrics from "Hands To Myself" by Selena Gomez.

In case you want to call a contact on your smartphone, you can ask Alexa to dial the contact and ask for his/her name and phone number. Again, you can ask for the name of a contact on your smartphone and Alexa will help you find it in the list of contacts. You can then just ask Alexa to call the contact.

Amazon Echo has more than a dozen Alexa skills available on its home screen. You can visit the "My Skills" page of your Alexa-powered speaker to see all the skills available on the Echo-powered speaker.

There is a separate "Skills Store" where you can find more than 10,000 skills. This section is the hub of all skills and skills. All skills in the Skills Store can be activated by asking Alexa to enable them.

For example, if you want to ask Alexa to search the Wikipedia page of "Bridesmaids," you can simply say "Alexa, open Wikipedia." Then you can search for the Bridesmaids movie on Wikipedia. Alexa will respond by saying that it will be enabled in 10 seconds. Then you just need to wait till Alexa finishes turning on the skill. Once the skill is enabled, you can ask Alexa to search the Bridesmaids movie on Wikipedia. Alexa will respond by saying that it will be enabled in two minutes. Now that's impressive. It only takes two minutes to enable a skill that will return any Wikipedia page to your Echo speaker.

You can also simply enable a skill by saying "Alexa, enable [skill name]."

The Amazon Echo is a device that's meant to be used as a daily companion. With a battery life of 15 hours, you can use the speaker for about 3-4 hours a day. The rest of the time, you'll just use the Alexa-powered speaker to listen to music, look up the weather, play a game or ask for news. Amazon's Alexa-powered speaker is no game-changer, but it is certainly useful as a companion.

What role of Alexa in business?

On top of everything else, there's the impact on commerce, such as home shopping and ordering. Ask most users about the most annoying experience they have had with a digital assistant, and it's in trying to order stuff. For Amazon Echo owners, the company gets a big cut of those sales.

For this reason, Amazon is focused on making Alexa more interactive for its customers, and rolling out new capabilities to make the shopping experience more enjoyable and convenient.

There are also the implications for other devices, such as smart thermostats. At CES in January, Amazon CEO Jeff Bezos noted Alexa has about ten times as many skills as the Google Assistant, which is Google's version of an assistant. This is one area where Google could still come out on top, given that the company already offers the Assistant for Google Home and other smart home devices, along with new features coming to more devices like Nest thermostats.

Meanwhile, Apple continues to do everything it can to get a foot in the door of the burgeoning smart home market, despite lagging in hardware compared to Amazon and Google. With the debut of Apple HomeKit, the Cupertino company is attempting to position Siri as a central player in that ecosystem. The next big battleground is the smart home speaker. This product category has the potential to change how we communicate with our devices, how we shop and how we experience the world.

What are Alexa secret tips?

To get Alexa to do a certain task, you have to say a certain phrase. However, Alexa will learn to do the job. Alexa usually will reply with a short voice prompt, such as "Alexa, open the sunroof", "Alexa, dim the lights", "Alexa, turn on some music" and similar, or with a voice command, such as "Alexa, ask Fabulous to play some music".

If the doorbell rings, you'll get Alexa to ask Fabulous to ring the doorbell. But when you say "Alexa, open the front door", you'll open the front door. This works with doorbells from a few manufacturers, including Ring.

For those who want to listen to the latest tracks on their Echo speaker, just say "Alexa, play E*Trade on Spotify". Alexa will send a request to Spotify for that particular song or artist, depending on where the album is stored.

The great thing is, once you've sent Spotify a command, Alexa will work to play the song. In the case of the E*Trade command, Alexa will open Spotify and send Spotify the request.

What can Alexa do for you when you're away from home?

Since Alexa has no screen, the assistant has a few tricks up its sleeve when you're away from home. It will record a message for you, so you'll receive a notification to say you've missed your family.

The assistant can turn on your Philips Hue smart bulbs so your home is lit when you arrive. Alexa can also be used to turn on your thermostat or flood and shower timer.

To stop your Amazon Echo device from waking up, just say "Alexa, don't wake me up."

You can ask Alexa to dim the lights, adjust the thermostat, and turn on your Philips Hue smart bulbs so your home is lit when you arrive. To stop your Amazon Echo device from waking up, just say "Alexa, don't wake me up."

How to use Alexa from a smartphone

Alexa can play music from streaming services such as Amazon Music, Spotify, and Pandora. For Apple users, the only music service Alexa supports is Apple Music. Spotify users can link their accounts to Alexa via the Alexa app.

If you don't have a smartphone with you, Alexa will play your music via TuneIn.

Other ways to use Alexa

If you have an Alexa device, but don't want to use it for shopping, you can use Alexa to control your Philips Hue smart lights. Alexa can turn your lights on or off, dim them, change colors, and control brightness levels.

If you don't have an Alexa device, but want to use it for shopping, you can use Alexa to control your Philips Hue smart lights. Alexa can turn your lights on or off, dim them, change colors, and control brightness levels. If you want to listen to music through your Sonos speakers, you can ask Alexa to play your favorite Spotify playlists or an album. Alexa can also play music from Amazon Music, Spotify, and Pandora, so Sonos music lovers can find songs that work best for them.

If you want to listen to music through your Sonos speakers, you can ask Alexa to play your favorite Spotify playlists or an album. Alexa can also play music from Amazon Music, Spotify, and Pandora, so Sonos music lovers can find songs that work best for them. Alexa will also let you order food from Amazon Fresh. Just say "Alexa, order pizza from Dominos" or "Alexa, order Chinese food".

How does Alexa relate to business?

So far, Alexa has mainly been integrated into Alexa-enabled

products like smart speakers or Amazon's line of Kindle tablets. But the digital assistant has also shown up in a handful of business-focused applications.

This year, the Washington State Department of Transportation (WSDOT) is piloting two pilots that integrate Alexa to help drivers. The first involves using Alexa to send text and email alerts to WSDOT drivers, alerting them to lane closures, other road hazards and congestion.

Another pilot combines Alexa with WSDOT's smartphone app to warn drivers of upcoming speed cameras. To do this, drivers will need to download the Alexa app, which will allow WSDOT to place Alexa on their phones and have the assistant automatically respond to speed camera notifications.

WSDOT spokesman Dave Goetz says the agency hopes that as the pilots are tested and scaled up, they could offer drivers useful traffic information — or be another reason for them to want to own a smart speaker.

"We want to show people that Alexa is a viable way for us

to provide real-time information to people," he says.

Making the most of Alexa in the workplace

To make Alexa more useful for work purposes, Goetz says WSDOT needs people to be familiar with the voice assistant and how to use it. This, he says, is an opportunity for some of the agency's workers.

"I think we can build up [the pilot program] from there, and provide training and information for our employees who are able to integrate Alexa with their work activities," he says.

But expanding beyond WSDOT's walls is a long way off. Alexa hasn't been certified as a remote assist for business — meaning it can't perform many of the tasks that are common in the workforce.

The challenge is figuring out which skills or features to

include, says Ryan Martin, a spokesman for Amazon, which owns Alexa.

"The most common applications and skills for Alexa in the workplace include retail and logistics," he says. "We've also seen the most use with commercial banks, the delivery companies and quick service restaurants — retailers like Starbucks, and quick-service restaurants like McDonald's."

"We've also seen the most use with commercial banks, the delivery companies and quick service restaurants — retailers like Starbucks, and quick-service restaurants like McDonald's."

Martin says Amazon is working with corporate customers to create Alexa skills that help businesses do things like manage inventory. He adds that Alexa can also be used in the home for skills like ordering flowers and setting timers.

"And we are just scratching the surface on all the capabilities and the ideas that people have with Alexa," he says. "We want to provide as many solutions and use cases as we possibly can."

Right now, the Alexa Skills Store only has about 50,000 individual skills, according to Martin. But he says there are tens of thousands of developers working on new Alexa skills, and he expects the company will continue to grow the number.

That doesn't necessarily mean the skills will be useful for people who work at their jobs — especially if they rely on technology.

Jennifer Hernandez, a technology researcher at the Center for Labor Research and Education at the University of California, Berkeley, says technology is often an afterthought in workplaces.

"In general, for employees in jobs like delivery workers or food servers or short-term retail workers — jobs that don't require a lot of skill or education — not only are there not a lot of benefits to [using Alexa at work], there's often not even the expectation that they should be working," she says.

Hernandez says that's something that's started to change recently.

"There are a lot of companies that are investing a lot in making their working environments more pleasant, they're doing things like offering free meals and a wide range of snacks," she says. "But they're not doing that for their workers in other aspects of the workplace."

She says the basic expectation at companies like Amazon and Uber is that employees are there to work — even if that means wearing a headset and talking to Alexa for hours at a time.

For some workers, it's difficult to switch off their focus from their job, Hernandez says.

"And, it's hard to sort of switch that off," she says. "It's hard to sort of check out of your work and sort of free yourself from that and be in a mindset of kind of — What am I going to have for dinner? What am I going to be doing that night?"

But if she ever gets an Alexa in her office, Hernandez says she might try using it a little.

Bridget Bentz, Molly Seavy-Nesper and Jeremy Farmer of the NPR Innovation Team contributed to this report.

Michelle Franzen is a multimedia reporter who covers workplace issues. This story is part of NPR's collaboration with KQED and Kaiser Health News.

Does Amazon Echo devices collect data?

Google and Amazon have very different approaches to customer privacy, with Google being much more forthcoming about what data it collects.

After the Cambridge Analytica scandal, you might be thinking about Google's stance on collecting data. To give you a brief overview, Google collects search queries. It then uses this to learn about you and offer personalized search results. This is one of the primary reasons you might use Google: because it does what you want it to. The downside is that Google is constantly collecting data. It's quite hard to opt out of the services Google offers because they are integrated so deeply in our day-to-day lives.

The US Federal Trade Commission has long taken a hands-off approach with Google, allowing the company to collect data on individual users. There is also a track record of non-compliance from Google with European regulators, as a 2014 settlement demonstrates.

However, Amazon doesn't disclose what data it collects about you or its products. In fact, it doesn't even acknowledge that it can do so under the law.

Amazon Echo, for example, can tell you the weather and provide news, but it cannot identify you when asked "Alexa, who am I?" Likewise, Echo and Echo Dot are unable to tell if you've given it the Echo or Echo Dot. It can't tell whether the house is empty or occupied, and won't respond if someone's voice is unknown.

Amazon could de-anonymize you

Many speakers on the market are equipped with microphone arrays. These allow it to listen to conversations and transcribe them to text. It can then use the transcriptions to learn more about you.

In theory, it could deduce that it is speaking to someone with the last name Jones and have the ability to confirm this. However, it would have to analyse the content of the audio transcript and create a "voiceprint" that could be used to identify an individual. Such analysis would be very time-consuming and expensive, however.

This is particularly true because it would have to assume that the Echo is hearing a random individual. There is no reason to believe this, given the fact that there are millions of people with identical voices. In fact, it's likely that Amazon would collect the voices of customers and friends.

Nevertheless, it is possible for speakers to de-anonymize users. For example, speakers using the Amazon Echo Dot may not be collecting enough audio data to learn about an individual. So while Echo could learn that the person speaking is in a household with other people in the household, it won't be able to determine who they are.

Google Home devices have considerably more powerful microphones than Echo Dot devices, and are able to learn audio profiles much more quickly. However, it is only able to do so if it hears the entire conversation. If the user asks, "OK Google, how tall is Timmy?" Google Home might assume that the owner of the account Timmy is the one asking the question, and not the other person.

If Google Home heard, for example, the last two questions, it would assume that there are two individuals and be able to deduce their genders. For this reason, users should think carefully before using speakers that have microphone arrays. It is possible for a device to learn about a person without their knowledge, and do so by taking in more data than necessary.

Google and Amazon are not the only companies interested in collecting your information. It is becoming increasingly popular for smart speakers to communicate with other devices. For example, the Amazon Echo could ask your Philips Hue smart light bulbs, "Who turned the lights on in the kitchen?" However, it can't ask the Philips Hue to tell Amazon exactly who turned the lights on.

The Google Home could also ask your Wemo connected smart plug, "Who is the master?" It couldn't ask the Wemo to pass on the information to Google. In other words, it couldn't de-anonymize you based on your lights.

The bottom line is that although smart speakers can learn a lot about you, it's a lot harder than it seems. These devices learn so much because they're designed to understand. There is a finite set of queries that a smart speaker is able to answer without any further assistance, and so much of their intelligence is based on how the device learns from the people using it.

However, this comes at a cost: The more it learns, the more it becomes similar to you and can reveal information that you might not want shared. If you care about your privacy, smart speakers shouldn't be your first stop when looking for a smart home product.

All the same, smart speakers are the most prominent smart home devices available and there is likely to be increased investment in this space in the future. The long-term success of these devices will depend on whether consumers feel comfortable using them, and how well they learn about them and their habits.

ALEXA

Chapter 1 What is Amazon Echo?

First things first: the Amazon Echo is a smart speaker. It can play music and stream podcasts via Amazon's own music service and also play radio stations, or you can tell Alexa to play the radio stations that are on TuneIn.

Now that that's out of the way, it's worth mentioning that the Amazon Echo also works with a variety of other smart-home systems including Wink, WeMo, Philips Hue, Nest, and Samsung SmartThings.

If you're not a fan of that "just say" trick, it can also be controlled with your phone - just say, "Alexa, turn on the lights" and Alexa will do so.

If you want to build a smart home, you can use the Amazon Echo to integrate your devices to make your home as smart as possible. You can do this by saying, "Alexa, enable the lights", or "Alexa, turn on the air conditioning", or "Alexa, dim the lights", or "Alexa, check the lights". All of these commands will work and Alexa will respond accordingly.

Just last week, Amazon also announced that, in addition to everything else it has, the Echo would be able to recognize your calendar, start a playlist or an alarm for when you're getting into your car and set a timer so you can prepare your morning coffee.

Amazon Echo is available in the US, UK, Germany, and Australia. In the US, the device costs $180. In the UK and Australia, it costs £130 (AU$235) and AU$199 (AU$320), respectively. In Germany and Austria, it costs €149 (AU$219).

Features

Looking at the features of Amazon Echo, you can tell it's not made by Google. Amazon is not at all shy about showing what it's made with its own ideas. But you don't have to be convinced by Amazon's bluster.

For one thing, the Amazon Echo has a great listening quality. It seems to have twice the bass and three times the treble of the Google Home and has a more balanced sound.

When music is playing, you can ask Alexa to adjust the volume, and she will respond immediately. Sometimes, she'll change the volume right away, but most of the time you'll need to tell her. However, Alexa isn't perfect with the music. If you ask her to turn on silence, she'll respond with a command such as "I can't change silence," or, "Silence is on".

However, you can tell her to turn on silence on Amazon's website by clicking on your Echo and selecting the settings icon.

And, if you ask Alexa to turn on the lights, the Echo will turn on the lights, and she'll work the lights by saying, "Alexa, turn on the lights". But she'll be able to start or stop the lights on your Ring Floodlight Cam by saying, "Alexa, turn on the lights" or "Alexa, turn on the porch light."

While you're with Alexa, you can ask her to read you the news, sports scores, and weather.

Amazon's Alexa device is also compatible with a lot of different smart-home systems.

Here's a list of some of the smart-home products that it can control with a simple voice command:

Wink - The Echo works with Wink, the smart-home system from Icontrol, but the Echo can also control the smart-home products from other companies such as August, TP-Link, Belkin, D-Link, GE, Insteon, Honeywell, Logitech, and Samsung SmartThings.

First Alert - First Alert makes a wide range of home security products and services including security cameras, smoke detectors, weather monitors, and more.

Philips Hue - The Echo works with Philips Hue, an in-home lighting system that's a connected lighting system that's built into lamps and other electronic devices. It can change the color of the lights you place around your home.

Nest - The Echo works with the Nest Learning Thermostat, a smart-home system that's made by Nest.

The Amazon Echo supports popular skills, but it also works with a small number of Alexa voice-activated apps.

Here's the current list of available skills, which are Alexa-based applications that allow you to do things like:

Entertainment - The Echo works with Amazon Prime Music, Amazon Music Unlimited, Audible, and TuneIn. It can also play audio from Spotify and Pandora.

News and Weather - The Echo works with the Amazon Prime News service, Weather.com, and Bing News.

Driving - The Echo works with Waze. You can get

directions on your phone, but if you want to give it a go yourself, you can ask Alexa to get directions from Waze on her own.

Routines - The Echo also works with routines. Routines allow you to say things such as, "Alexa, I'm home," to have the Echo turn on your lights, close the shades, adjust the thermostat, and play music.

Voice commands

Alexa's built-in voice-command capabilities are pretty limited. You can use your voice to:

- Play a song (or a genre of songs) from Amazon Music, iHeartRadio, Spotify, Pandora, SiriusXM Internet Radio, and TuneIn.
- Listen to the weather forecast from AccuWeather or The Weather Channel.
- Change the volume on your TV, audio system, or speakers.

- Change the channel on your TV or sound system.
- Set the volume on your speaker, if it's connected via a cable.
- Change the channel on your stereo, if it's connected via a cable.
- Change the channel on your tablet, if it's connected via a cable.
- Open your favorite news, sports, or weather apps.
- Turn the TV off.
- Turn the TV on.
- Turn the lights off or on (if connected with a smart-home device).
- Change the volume of the TV or audio system.
- Turn the heat/air conditioning on/off (if connected via a smart-home device).
- Search the web.
- Set reminders, due dates, and alarms.
- Create new reminders.
- Stop an alarm (if it's connected via a smart-home device).
- Change the alarm tone on your smartphone or tablet.
- Open the Alexa app.
- Open the Google Assistant app.
- Stop an alarm on your smartphone or tablet.
- Change the alarm tone on your smartphone or tablet.
- Change the wake word (if you have more than one).

- Make an audible to remind yourself to get up and take your medicine.
- Make a "Go to sleep" alarm.
- Turn off the lights.
- Scroll through photos in the Alexa app (or just say, "Alexa, show me my photos.").

When can I buy an Echo?

It's still in the early days, but it's available right now for pre-order.

How much does an Echo cost?

A few dollars are less than the equivalent Sonos speaker.

Do I have to pay for an Amazon Prime membership?

Not necessarily, though the Echo currently requires an Amazon Prime membership, which comes with a bunch of benefits.

Does the Echo work with my smartphone?

Right now, you can get Alexa on most smartphones and tablets that use Android 4.0 and above, or iOS 9 and above. That list includes the Samsung Galaxy S5, LG G4, the Moto X, the ZTE Axon 7, the Amazon Fire Phone, and, for now, the Amazon Fire tablets. Amazon also offers an Alexa app for the Amazon Fire HD 8 tablet.

Do I need to add an Amazon Prime membership to my

order?

No, but Prime members get a few additional perks. You can cancel your membership at any time, and you get two-day shipping, plus Amazon Prime Video, Prime Music, and other perks.

Does an Echo need a power outlet?

Not necessarily, though the Echo has to be connected to power. There are ways to make sure you don't run out of juice, but you should check Amazon's website to learn more.

What smart-home devices can I use with the Echo?

The Echo works with a ton of connected devices. You can link different products through an Amazon Echo app or your existing smart-home hub. Some of the supported smart-home devices include Philips Hue lighting, WeMo, iHome Smart Speakers, Logitech Harmony, Honeywell Lyric, Alarm.com, Flic Connected Thermostat, Crestron Home Entertainment Systems, a Sonos speaker, Philips Hue bulbs, and more.

Can I use multiple Echos together?

No, but you can assign a number to each Echo device. For example, I have a list on my Echo that says "Alexa, show me the garage door." If you have more than one Echo device, you can only have one "show me the garage door."

So, what's the difference between the Amazon Echo and the Amazon Echo Dot?

The Echo has a 360-degree speaker, so it can play music and have voice assistants. The Echo Dot has a 2.5-inch woofer and a 1.6-inch tweeter for sound. The Amazon Echo comes with a base with a built-in speaker, but the Dot comes with a traditional charging station with a powered, uni-body design. The Echo also costs $179, while the Echo Dot costs $50. The Echo Dot does get you more voice-assistant skills, though.

Where can I buy an Echo?

The Echo is available for pre-order now, and the Echo Dot is available now for order, but they won't ship until June 27.

How much do I have to pay for an Echo?

In order to pre-order, you'll need to pay $179 for an Echo,

but you'll only pay $99 after June 27, 2016. The Amazon Echo is available for pre-order now, and the Echo Dot is available now for order, but they won't ship until June 27.

Where can I buy an Echo?

The Echo will be available for pre-order on Amazon.com, Amazon.co.uk, and in the U.K. Amazon.co.uk will sell the Echo at the same price as the U.S. version. If you're outside of the U.S., you'll need to enter your country and language to see the price difference.

What other Alexa-enabled devices are available?

Echo works with any connected speaker that has an infrared blaster. That means the Amazon Echo works with the full line of Sonos speakers, and the Echos can also be paired with a variety of other connected products. There are dozens of products that work with Amazon Alexa, and you can even connect an Echo to your Bluetooth speaker to turn the speaker into a standalone Alexa device.

Is there a way to use Google Assistant?

Yes, but it's much more limited. The Echo does not work with Google Home devices, and Google has no plans to support it. You can also use the Google Home with the Google Assistant app on your Android or iOS device.

On Android, you need to enable the Google Home skill in the Google Home app and then link it with your Google account. Google Assistant works best with devices that you can talk to directly, which is why you'll need to link an Echo to your account in order to use Google Assistant. You can still control Google Assistant with an Echo using the Amazon Alexa app.

Why isn't Alexa available in the UK?

Amazon doesn't offer Echo devices in the U.K., and it can be a challenge to make the U.K. compatible with Alexa because the language is based on British English, not American English.

Should I get an Echo for my kids?

All smart speakers make kids nervous. No, they're not smart speakers. They're always listening. And if you want to know if they're listening, you can always ask Alexa, "Alexa, do you love me?" Because Alexa isn't an open standard like Apple's Siri, there isn't a way to hear how the devices are being used, so they could always be recording and saving audio to listen to later. For that reason, I wouldn't let kids use the Echo or any other Alexa-enabled device for a while.

Is Alexa safe?

It's extremely hard to hack into an Echo. Just like you wouldn't give your laptop or phone to a child, you shouldn't let your children buy an Echo. You can buy an Amazon Echo in the U.S. and Amazon Alexa in the U.K. You'll need to buy your Echo from Amazon in order to set it up and use it, so if you're buying it from Amazon's website, you're buying it from Amazon itself. The Echo is covered by the same warranty as a Kindle, so if something happens, you're covered.

Should I buy the smaller Echo Dot instead of the full-sized Echo?

The Echo Dot is smaller and it's more portable. It's also cheaper. At $50 (or £50 or about $AU60), the Echo Dot is $10 cheaper than the full-sized Echo, and it works with the same speaker and so it's just as powerful. It's the smart speaker for people who don't want to commit to a whole-house sound system.

Is it worth it to buy a second Echo for music?

Yes. It's cheaper than having an Echo Dot and a separate Amazon Music subscription. Amazon offers two-year subscriptions for $3.99 (about £2.80 or AU$4.60), and the Echo Dot is the closest thing to an Echo you can put anywhere in the house, so you don't even need a dedicated Echo speaker in every room. You can also ask Alexa to play music in your living room without it being loud because it still has the same speaker.

What other smart speakers are out there?

The Apple HomePod is not out yet, but it will cost $349 when it arrives in December, which is nearly $100 more than the Amazon Echo.

What apps does Alexa support?

Alexa is compatible with tens of thousands of third-party apps, from the free. She can play music, set a timer, and order an Uber, just like the Google Assistant.

Should I buy a smart speaker?

Yes, for lots of reasons. Amazon Echo will be a centerpiece of your smart home. You can use it to check the weather, set a timer, control your smart home devices and order you some cold brew at 4 a.m. You can even order a pizza.

Chapter 2 What benefits of Amazon Echo?

Amazon Echo is currently one of the most promising products in the home automation domain. Amazon Echo integrates with Alexa, a virtual personal assistant. Alexa allows the Amazon Echo devices to do an easy job at your home.

Alexa is similar to Siri, a virtual personal assistant, only that Alexa has a conversational interface. Also, Alexa can understand voice commands and perform requests very easily. Also, Alexa works with Amazon Echo, Amazon Echo Dot, Amazon Echo Show, and Amazon Tap. Alexa voice assistant works through the Internet, not Bluetooth.

Alexa can perform many things, but let us see how Alexa works and what benefits Alexa Echo.

How does Alexa work?

Amazon Echo has a built-in speaker to play music from a local music library or from Spotify, Pandora, Amazon Prime Music, Deezer, etc. But, if you are using Amazon Echo, Amazon Echo Dot, Amazon Echo Show, you can stream audio from the internet.

Alexa is built-in to your device and it connects through a 3.5mm audio jack and uses your home Wi-Fi. You can use Alexa for a number of things, which we will see in this post.

Alexa can answer questions or give answers to questions. You can use Amazon Echo to control your smart lights, thermostat, lock system, etc. It is not only a smart hub, it can also control the cable box from the TV and cable or home security camera.

Alexa, the personal assistant lets you get information, but Alexa can also take over your life.

Alexa can control the temperature in the house, lights, lock system, TV, keep a check on traffic and daily news. But, Alexa is not limited to home automation, Alexa can control everything. Alexa can send and receive messages from your Alexa-enabled device to other Alexa-enabled devices.

You can use Alexa to control your thermostat, lights, lock system, TV, set the temperature. Alexa can turn on the air conditioning system, open the windows or lock the doors.

Alexa can be used to make Alexa Calls to any number of phone numbers. Alexa can perform a few basic tasks like controlling your music player or setting your alarm, but you can use Alexa for everything at your home. Alexa can answer questions and send SMS messages. It can read the news, play audio files or read text messages. You can use Alexa to set an alarm or a timer for cooking. Alexa can give you the local weather, let you know the traffic, and so on.

Setting Up Amazon Echo

Setting up Amazon Echo is not difficult at all. Amazon Echo is a small device, which looks like an old IP phone. You have to plug the Echo into an HDMI port of your TV and use an HDMI cable to connect the Echo with your network. The Echo has an LED display with a blue light, which comes on automatically when you turn on your TV, and then the Echo lights up.

The first thing you will have to do is, to pair the Amazon Echo with the Internet. This is a fairly easy task and you don't need to have an Internet connection to use Amazon Echo. All you need is a Wi-Fi connection to get started. If you don't have a Wi-Fi connection, you can get a wired connection or a mobile data connection.

1. Open the Alexa App from the App Store or Google Play Store.
2. In the App, click the settings icon.
3. Make sure you are on the same network with the Amazon Echo.
4. After you have entered your Wi-Fi details, click Pair now.
5. After a few seconds, the Amazon Echo will automatically be connected to the Wi-Fi network.
6. The next step is, you need to update the Alexa App. Open the App, then tap the update button.

7. When you see the update screen, tap the Download and Install button.

8. In the Install Files screen, you need to click on Update All. After updating the app, you can now set up the Echo device.

Setting up Alexa In Your Car

The Amazon Echo can be used in your car too. It has Bluetooth 4.1 and operates using a car's USB port. Connect your Echo to the USB port in your car. You need to turn on Bluetooth. If you do not see the icon on the car's dashboard, you need to make sure the car is started. You will find a small light on the Echo. Once the car is on, you will be able to use Alexa. This makes the Echo the most portable Amazon Echo ever. If you have a navigation device with a display, such as Garmin or TomTom, you can use Alexa to give your car directions. This way, you don't have to worry about making turns or changing lanes.

If you have an Alexa-enabled device, you can give directions, but you can also use Alexa while driving. You can use Alexa to keep a check on traffic, answer questions, look up information, and so on.

Setting Up Alexa For A Child

One of the most impressive things about Amazon Echo is that Alexa has been designed with a child in mind. Alexa can be used by kids in many ways. You can use Alexa to play music, read stories, set timers, and so on. Alexa can also control the smart devices in your home. Here is a list of some of the things you can do with your Alexa-enabled device.

Alexa can read stories to your kids. You can tell Alexa to "read a story to me" and she will read a story for you, in an adult voice.

You can ask Alexa to turn on the TV, a projector, or a Kindle.

You can ask Alexa to tell your kids a bedtime story or give them a bath.

You can ask Alexa to tell you a joke.

If you have a Philips Hue light bulb in your home, you can use Alexa to control the lights, even when you are not at home.

Use your voice to dim the lights or set them to a specific color.

You can ask Alexa to turn on or off the central air conditioning.

Alexa can tell you the news, weather, or traffic.

You can use your voice to call a taxi, order food from an

app, or create a playlist.

Alexa is now part of the smart home. You can use Alexa to dim the lights, change the thermostat or turn on the heat. You can also use Alexa to monitor your home security. You can set up your Amazon Echo as a "smart hub" and control the lights, locks, thermostat, security cameras, and other smart devices with just your voice.

Setting Up Alexa For Anyone

For any individual who has a smart home, Amazon Echo is a must-have gadget. As Amazon says, Alexa is the most versatile virtual assistant. In any case, Amazon Echo does not replace your smartphone or tablet. It has different uses. You can use Alexa to control your smart devices, your thermostat, music, and more. You can also use Alexa to call a taxi, book a table in a restaurant, and so on. If you want to watch videos or play games, you can use the Echo to do that too. It makes a perfect gift for anyone who loves the idea of an always-on virtual assistant.

Amazon Echo can be used for multiple things. It can be used as a smart speaker, a voice-controlled music player, a security device, remote control, and more. You can use Amazon Echo to make your smart home more secure.

Using Alexa On An Android Phone

Using Alexa on an Android smartphone is also simple. All you need to do is download the Alexa app and set it up. You can pair your smartphone to your Echo using the Amazon Echo app.

Once you set up Alexa on your smartphone, you can use Alexa to control your smart home, get updates on news, weather and traffic, control your smart devices, make a call, ask questions, set alarms, add items to your shopping list, and so on.

Summary

Smart homes are the next big thing. By making your home a smart home, you will be able to manage all of your home's smart devices and manage your home smartly. When your home is a smart home, you can also use Alexa to play music, watch videos, control the lights and thermostat, and so on.

Although there is no bad news for smart homeowners, it is important to understand that smart home products may get better and better. With such products, you can create the ultimate smart home.

This means you can use Alexa to do the things that Amazon Echo is not capable of doing, and you will be able to add other smart products to your home.

Chapter 3 How to set up Amazon Echo?

Setting up Amazon Echo is easy. The only additional step you have to take is to link the Echo device to your Amazon account.

In the Alexa app, open the menu and click on the Devices button at the top of the screen. Next, click on Link a Device.

Enter your Amazon Echo, followed by a PIN and a four-digit phrase that only you know.

When you hear Alexa speak, simply say: "Alexa, open Echo."

You can also link any of your smart home devices and stream music, news, and podcasts on your Amazon Echo. To do so, open the Alexa app, tap on the Devices button, and scroll to the bottom of the page where it says Link a

Device.

Alexa will automatically scan your Wi-Fi network, detect the devices in your house, and associate each device with the appropriate name. Once that's done, simply enable the device and click the Devices button to enter your PIN and phrase.

If you already have Alexa devices set up in your home, this should take you less than a minute to set up your new Echo. If not, follow our guide on how to set up an Alexa device.

How to use Amazon Echo?

Just as you can with any other Alexa device, you can use Amazon Echo to check the weather, listen to music, order an Uber, and so much more.

To do so, first, open the Alexa app on your phone and

follow the instructions to download the skill for the feature you're interested in. To do so, open the Alexa app, go to the Skills section, and then tap on the desired skill to open it.

Next, tap on the Skills button in the upper-right corner. You'll see a list of Alexa skills on the screen, and the option to Add this Skill button on the far-right.

Tap on the Add button to bring up a window that will allow you to enter the skill name, and the trigger phrase (in this case, "Alexa, open Echosaurus Rex").

Follow the instructions to set up the skill and Alexa will activate it once it's downloaded on your phone.

Now, you'll be able to use it to play music and news from NPR One or any of the other news sources you add to your Alexa skills.

If you'd like to try out Alexa's new Dash Wand, simply open the Alexa app and tap on the Dash Wand icon.

Alexa will automatically scan the Wi-Fi network, and you can add any grocery items you'd like to your shopping list, as well as set a timer for your popcorn.

You can also use Alexa to check the weather, get directions, play a movie or podcast, and much more.

Alexa's new Skills API can give the device new and unique capabilities.

Amazon recently launched the Alexa Skills API, which will let developers create custom Alexa skills. These are simple, flash-based apps that allow people to control smart home devices and do a myriad of other things with the voice command of "Alexa."

According to Amazon, that's just the beginning:

"The Alexa Skills Kit is the first step toward realizing our vision of a world where any skill can be initiated by voice. A growing community of developers and entrepreneurs are contributing to this vision with their skills and the support and encouragement of Amazon. And now, with the launch of the Alexa Skills Kit API, it's easy for anyone to create these skills in minutes. This includes custom skills that support the many features of Amazon Echo-like music playback, automated timers, news, entertainment, and more."

Families, roommates, and friends can use Amazon Echo to play games and quiz each other.

Perhaps one of the most unique uses for Amazon Echo is in the home. Many Alexa owners have paired the device with their smartphones to create a multi-person Echo that listens for the wake word, Alexa, and then responds to any requests.

To do so, simply pair your Amazon Echo with the Alexa app, then go to the Devices page and select the Echo you'd like to pair with your phone. It's as simple as that.

And because your phone is involved, you can play games with your friends and family. Just pair an Echo and your phone, then find a game you'd both enjoy.

For example, if you want to play a game, you could ask your Echo, "Alexa, play Jeopardy with Charli," and then they'd both take turns playing Jeopardy! by asking Alexa trivia questions and then typing their answers into the Alexa App.

The best part of using this feature is that your answers are private, and only the two of you can see your answers.

And you can also do even more fun things like play a game of soccer, take turns beating each other at chess or even send your other person voice memos.

The biggest downside of using an Alexa and smartphone combo, however, is that it can be difficult to communicate when both people are using their phones.

Locations are an especially useful tool for travelers.

As a frequent traveler, I've used my Amazon Echo to book a hotel room, answer my phone, and even order food in the middle of a crowded restaurant.

Locations, a feature within the Alexa app, makes it incredibly easy to find whatever you're looking for.

As you use the Alexa app to navigate through its various features, you can ask Alexa, "Alexa, where can I find a panda in San Francisco?" And Alexa will tell you that there is a panda on AT&T Park. Alexa can also turn on the flashlight on your phone and listen to your voice commands.

Amazon has added several new features to Alexa that are all aimed at making the voice assistant better for you and your friends and family. And it's only going to get better from here.

An Amazon Echo Plus is your best friend.

If you want to make your house smarter, start by getting an Amazon Echo Plus. The Alexa-enabled smart speaker is as big as two plates of shrimp and comes with a built-in smart hub. It can tell the difference between music you're playing on an Amazon Echo and music from a smart TV or stereo. And it can order things for you – like groceries or dog food – when you ask it to.

Plus, if you have multiple Amazon Echo Plus devices in your house, you can group them together and control them all from one Echo Plus.

My favorite feature about Amazon Echo Plus, however, is its screen. When you ask Alexa to show you a playlist of songs, it can play a sample of the music and display song lyrics. That's right, you can talk to Alexa without having to turn on your phone and switch between screens.

Amazon Echo Dots are now $20 less expensive.

Echo Dot speakers, which aren't actually smart speakers, but just Amazon's Alexa assistant, are usually listed at $50, but the device's price has just dropped by $20.

This is great news for anyone who wants to buy an Echo Dot as a gift for a loved one.

All you have to do is say, "Alexa, order a Google Home Mini for [birthday person's name]."

The price drop means you can get a nice new smart speaker, plus two Echo Dots, for the price of one.

Ordering in with Alexa is a breeze.

If you're a Prime member, you can order your groceries, a new TV, or your dog food with just your voice.

When you order from Amazon's Alexa app, you can add items to your cart and reorder them whenever you're running low on supplies. You can even set timers.

Once your shopping cart is ready, you can ask Alexa to

check it out for you.

However, if you ask Alexa to put items in your cart, Amazon will give you a 5-minute window to do so, and you have to place the order with your voice. So, you can't place multiple orders at the same time.

You can also make purchases on your Amazon Echo.

If you can't wait five minutes to place your next order, you can make purchases using your voice with Amazon Echo.

What basic settings for Alexa?

The Echo range comes with a default profile that can be changed to a different one in a similar way, just by enabling the settings available in Settings. The basic settings are the following:

General settings:

Change wake word – this is either Alexa or Amazon. The voice ID may be set to either.

Show name on top – The name of the device is shown on top of the device and can also be selected in order to easily differentiate between Alexa and Echo.

Settings:

Music – Allows you to select your default music player, default music service, and allows you to enable/disable shuffle.

Echo – This allows you to access the basic Alexa functions as in Settings section above.

Alerts – Allows you to enable/disable other Alexa notifications.

Skills – This option is available for users who wish to enable/disable the third-party Alexa Skills. Alexa can also be installed on other devices but this feature is unavailable at the moment.

Behaviour and applications:

Alexa skills – It is the third-party Alexa applications that allow you to accomplish several tasks on your Echo device. Here the list of the Alexa Skills can be found.

Alexa for Business – One of the Alexa Features for Business is this feature that enables you to interact with a business or other organization that already has an Alexa skill for Alexa.

Other features:

Voice Memos – Record your voice notes.

Get started with your device – This will guide you in the direction of Alexa, without requiring you to login on any other website.

Device history – This shows you all the commands, questions and user responses that you have given to Alexa.

Unlocked state – Allows you to enable/disable accessing of Alexa features if you aren't in the Echo range.

Device classes – Sets the particular device into one of the class like Amazon Music, Philips Hue, Dropcam, etc.

Audible, Music and News – These can be changed individually.

Location based services:

Alexa Location – This allows you to make use of Alexa's location and track her location as per your wishes.

Wobble motion sensor – This turns on Alexa's backlight when the device is moved in front of her.

Keyboard pin – This will enable you to enable or disable the Bluetooth keyboard.

Amazon is also launching an application called the Skills Kit to allow developers to create Alexa skills.

Voice controlled device Alexa leads the Smart Home industry and has so far scored a lot of popularity among its customers. The speaker currently has hundreds of third-party skills in its repertoire and this is a solid competitor to

Google Home.

Moreover, the development of smart devices has gained momentum recently with an increase in sales of such products. This is definitely one of the strongest advantages of the Amazon Echo in this regard. The massive growth in popularity of Alexa, has left Google Home in a distant third place. This has caused many to believe that Google may launch its own smart speaker to challenge the Amazon Echo.

Google Home is not available in the United States. While the Echo is widely available, Google Home is not. It is expected to be launched in this market in November. However, it is currently available in India for Rs 11,999, for Indian users.

The Amazon Echo now costs $179 in the United States and in India. This means that the Echo costs Rs 35,272. However, that is a little high. Amazon is also available on other platforms including Windows 10 and Mac OS.

Chapter 4 What are Alexa skills?

Amazon recently added additional voice-activated capabilities to its Echo speakers. The Amazon Echo is a battery-powered cylinder, about a foot in diameter, that comes with a 7-inch screen. It can be placed anywhere in a room and can connect to speakers that are in other rooms.

For Alexa users, the device is filled with various "skills," or apps, that allow it to do more than just play music and tell you the news.

But to get started with Alexa, users must enable the device on their account, select a few skills, and then set up the device in the Alexa app on their phone. Afterward, the new Alexa app will alert you with an OOMPAG announcement alerting you that your skills are ready for use.

Amazon's Alexa allows users to search for information, get weather forecasts, set alarms and timers, look up recipes, and play games. There are also thousands of other skills that allow the device to perform certain functions.

With the Skill Blueprints, users can generate unique voice capabilities by creating a list of objects they want Alexa to understand. Once the necessary skills are added, users can teach the skill, ask Alexa to say specific words, or even create a phrase with a specific meaning.

If this is your first time using Alexa on your phone, here's how to get started:

Go to the Alexa app on your Android or iOS device. Click on the search icon and enter the name of the Alexa Skill you want to create. Click the Create skill button. Enter a name for the skill. Tap Create Skill.

Once you set up your smart home devices, Alexa will respond to voice commands. "Alexa, what can I do?" is the obvious way to get the ball rolling, but you'll quickly discover there are countless "skills" on the Alexa platform.

Eager to learn about them? Here's everything you need to know about smart home skills.

How to get smart home skills

First up, the most important bit. When you want to add a new skill to Alexa, you can do so from the Amazon Alexa app on Android or iOS (both):

Tap the menu button in the top-right corner Tap Skills Tap Skills & Devices Tap Skills & Devices Once you've found a skill you want, tap the arrow button and follow the instructions

From there, you can add it to your queue or tap the toggle to use it right away. When you hear a voice prompt, tap the skill, which can be enabled or disabled, and you can ask for help to activate it. Once it's activated, you can then ask Alexa for everything from news and weather to the average price of gas and how many customers Amazon has in California.

How to install a smart home skill

If you just want to find out about all the new skills that are being released, we've got you covered. Here's how to install a new skill:

Open the Alexa app Click the menu button (three horizontal lines in the top-left corner) Tap Skills Tap Skills & Devices Tap Skills > Skills > New Skill

Find a skill you want, tap the arrow button and follow the instructions.

Once you've completed the skill's steps, it'll be ready to use. You can now use your voice to ask for it.

How to delete a skill

If you're not particularly excited about a particular smart home skill, there's a way to get rid of it, as long as you have the skill installed:

Open the Alexa app Click the menu button (three horizontal lines in the top-left corner) Select the top navigation bar and choose Settings Tap Skills Tap Skills & Devices Tap Skills > Skills & Devices Select Remove Skill Select Yes and follow the instructions

From there, the skill will be removed from your list and you'll have to re-install it.

Once a skill is installed, it's generally associated with a single Alexa account, so it will be removed from a new device once you change your profile.

Learn more

If you want to learn more about a particular smart home skill, or find a more "how-to" for a particular skill, here are some resources:

Knowing how to use smart home skills

Once you've set up your smart home devices, the fun begins, but first, it's time to learn how to use your new devices to accomplish basic tasks.

Chapter 5 What are Amazon Echo devices?

Amazon's Echo devices let you use your voice to access Alexa's knowledge and power. You can use the Echo to play music, order food from Amazon, play games, set alarms, control connected appliances, shop, and even control smart home devices. In other words, you don't have to be a technical genius to use Alexa's abilities.

The Echo, Echo Dot, and Echo Plus all feature 7-inch or larger touch screens so you can tap, swipe and pinch to navigate around the screen. You can also ask Alexa questions. She can answer "real" questions and concerns, too, like the weather, traffic, what's on tonight's TV, sports scores and much more.

If you've got an Amazon Echo device in your house you'll probably be interested in Amazon Music Unlimited. Available on the Echo and Echo Dot, the Unlimited music streaming service offers unlimited ad-free access to tens of millions of songs, to music you already own, or to any songs you want to create a personalized "radio" station with. Spotify, Pandora, and Google Play are all included, too. You also get access to Alexa skills and other exclusive content, too.

Similar to Apple's iTunes and iCloud service, Amazon Music Unlimited doesn't require a subscription. All you need to do is buy one single month or one three month subscription, and the rest is included. But if you do decide to stick with a subscription you'll always be able to start a new one for as little as $7.99 per month, or one for $99 per year.

You can also use Alexa on your smartphone or tablet to access Alexa's voice recognition skills. These let you activate your Echo by saying, "Alexa, open [name of a skill]" and using the supplied microphone. The Amazon Music app on Android and iOS can also be used to access Alexa.

For example, you can say, "Alexa, ask Uber to request a ride," or "Alexa, ask Domino's to start a two-hour delivery," or even, "Alexa, ask Pandora to play the A Cautionary Tale by Death Cab for Cutie." Alexa also lets you play music from Amazon Music Unlimited if you're signed into your Amazon account on another device, too.

Additional Echo devices aren't essential for using Alexa's skills, but it's useful to have them around if you want to set up a multi-room music system, or a set of smart lights. The Philips Hue bulbs can be linked to an Echo so you can just shout commands like, "Alexa, dim the bedroom lights to 30 percent."

Can Alexa help with my shopping list?

The Echo Spot and Echo Dot both include Alexa-compatible displays, so you can show or read what you're shopping for. If you have more than one Echo device, you can set up a "voice shopping list" where you can say, "Alexa, add eggs to my shopping list," or "Alexa, add vegetables to my shopping list."

As for Alexa skills, you can find new ones by asking for a specific skill. In addition to the services we mentioned earlier, the following Skills let you order things:

- Amazon Restaurants
- eBay
- Habitat
- Home Advisor
- Johnson & Johnson Consumer
- Jet.com
- Kroger
- Living Social
- Mother's Miracle Network
- Manhattan Motors
- Monoprice
- Petsmart
- Pavlok
- Shell
- Staples
- Target

The app on your phone or tablet will need to be connected to your account. You then use your phone or tablet to scan the barcode of the items you need and the items will be ordered.

How do I set up my Echo?

Setting up your Echo is easy. Just download the free Alexa app for either your iPhone or Android, or if you're using an Echo Dot or Echo Spot.

When you first fire up the app, you'll be asked to choose your country, then connect to your Amazon account. Once you've got those two done, you'll be ready to set up your Echo device.

On the first page of the app you'll find information about Alexa, including a description of the Echo, basic information about the Echo speaker, and instructions on how to set up your Echo. You can also customize your home speaker's name, music playback settings, wake word, and more.

Next you'll see the Devices tab, where you can link the Echo to your home network, and pair it to your other devices. You can see a list of compatible smart home devices on the Devices tab, including the Philips Hue smart bulbs. To enable Alexa to connect to your connected devices, just tap the Devices tab and select Devices. Then scroll down until you see the smart home hub you'll need to connect to. In our case, we connected to an Logitech

Harmony Hub, so we can control all of the various devices in our home using the Alexa Voice Service.

You'll next see the Scenes section. Here you can create a new scene that will trigger Alexa to start listening for the wake word. You can add a sound to the scene, and also can add a video or photo from your device to the scene.

After you create your scene, tap Next to add it to the Alexa app. You'll be taken to a screen where you can set a name for the scene and fill in a caption. Tap Continue to make the scene live.

You'll next be prompted to connect to your home Wi-Fi, so Alexa can start listening for the wake word. After you set up the Wi-Fi, you can tap Next to save the scene, and also give it a description and a description and caption for Alexa to read aloud.

Next, you'll see a screen where you can set your default location for your device, so Alexa can always understand your voice and will always respond when you're in your home. You can change your default location by tapping Change Settings, and then tap either Create a new location, or Add a new location.

For the next step, you'll be taken to the Settings page for your Alexa device. Here you can enable the device to work as an accessibility device, so Alexa will listen for your command even when there's no word for that command.

Finally, you'll see the Devices screen, where you can see the devices in your home.

How do I listen to music on my Echo?

Music playback on your Echo is a feature that's been available on the Amazon Music app for a while, but that's not the only way to listen to music on your device. You can listen to your music stored in the Amazon Cloud Drive, or even listen to your music and radio stations from TuneIn, iHeartRadio, Pandora, or Slacker Radio.

To listen to music stored on the Amazon Cloud Drive, open the Alexa app, then tap the Devices button. In the Devices screen, tap the Devices option and select your

Echo from the list. Scroll down to the Music and Services section and select the Music tab.

In the Music Services section, you can add a Music Services account by tapping the Add a Music Services account option, and entering your Amazon account email and password. When prompted, choose your Amazon Cloud Drive and grant the Music Services account access to your music. You can also download music from any supported music service to your device, and it's compatible with Amazon Music, Spotify, iHeartRadio, Pandora, and more.

If you don't have any music stored in the Amazon Cloud Drive, you can also access music from your device's list of local music on your Amazon Music account. Tap the devices icon in the Music Services section, and select your device from the list. In the Music Services section, you can browse through the available music services.

How do I play music?

Playing music is one of the most important features on the Echo. You can play music from a connected music service or directly from your Amazon Music library, by using the built-in music playback controls on your device. To play music, tap the music player icon on the top left of the device screen.

The music player screen is similar to what you see in an Echo speaker, and is just a different way to control playback. You can play, pause, skip forward and back, and even adjust the volume of the music playback by tapping the playback controls on the right side of the device screen.

What can I ask Alexa to do?

There are a lot of things you can ask Alexa, and the best part is that you don't need to tap any of the mic icons to get results. From music playback controls to smart home controls to setting timers, you can ask Alexa to do a lot of things.

Here are some examples of what you can ask your Echo:

"Alexa, when is the Super Bowl?" "Alexa, is it time to leave for work?" "Alexa, set a timer for 5 minutes." "Alexa, turn on the house lights." "Alexa, what was the weather like today?" "Alexa, set a timer for 3 minutes." "Alexa, turn on the bedroom lights." "Alexa, what is the temperature outside?" "Alexa, play some jazz music." "Alexa, is my alarm set for 7:30?" "Alexa, turn on the TV." "Alexa, what time is it?" "Alexa, play some basketball music." "Alexa, what was the score of last night's game?" "Alexa, how long have I been asleep?" "Alexa, tell me a joke." "Alexa, set a timer for 10 minutes." "Alexa, what is the weather like tomorrow?" "Alexa, stop the alarms." "Alexa, add an alarm to my calendar." "Alexa, order me some flowers." "Alexa, set a timer for 5 minutes." "Alexa, change my alarm tone to be fun." "Alexa, set a timer for 5 minutes." "Alexa, put on some music." "Alexa, show me a recipe I can make." "Alexa, set a timer for 15 minutes." "Alexa, play some slow jam music." "Alexa, play some music from the 1970s." "Alexa, set a timer for 5 minutes." "Alexa, add the recipe for beef stew to my shopping list." "Alexa, add a recipe to my shopping list." "Alexa, add a recipe to my shopping list." "Alexa, make sure my coffee maker is set for coffee." "Alexa, set the thermostat to 68 degrees." "Alexa, set my timer for 15 minutes."

Keep in mind that Amazon will give you an unexpected result or answer the last question. If you ask something that isn't really relevant to your query, you may get an unexpected result. Amazon collects all of the unplanned results and uses them to improve Alexa. To learn more about the ways Alexa collects information, read How Amazon Smarts.

What can I ask Alexa to read to me?

When you ask Alexa to read to you, you can have it read out e-books, Kindle ebooks, or any other book on your connected device, like Audible.

For Alexa to read, you need to give it access to a Kindle library and enable the Alexa skill on the connected device.

How do I get more features on Alexa?

More features can be added to Alexa as you discover new skills. To find a new skill, tap the Alexa app icon on your home screen, then select the icon that looks like a star and select Skills.

If you want to know more about the new feature, you can tap the information icon below the Skill you want to know more about. To see all of the features available on Alexa, tap the All Skills icon on your home screen.

Is Alexa available in other countries?

Yes. Alexa is currently available in the US, UK, Germany, France, Canada, Australia, and Japan.

However, there are still some Alexa skills that are only available in the US. For example, there are still Echo skills that require Flash or require an internet connection, even though those features have been removed from the Alexa app. For example, flash is still available in the US.

How can I get help?

To get help with any question or question, you can tap the microphone icon on your home screen, then click on Settings to choose help or Suggest a Skill.

If you are looking for a specific skill, you can go directly to its page in the Skills section.

I'm using an Echo speaker or an Alexa-enabled device. How can I connect to Alexa using my phone?

You can connect to Alexa using your phone as long as you are using the same account.

To do so, you will need to sign in using your Amazon account. You will also need to grant the Alexa app permission to access your microphone, access your contact list, and to make location-based voice requests.

Click here to learn more about setting up Alexa-enabled devices with your phone.

Is Alexa available to kids?

Amazon's Alexa is a voice-controlled device for everyone, but that does not mean children should be excluded from the fun.

You can give Alexa a job, such as setting alarms, playing music, reading stories, or adding items to your shopping list.

To set up and enable the Echo Dot Kids Edition, go to amazon.com/echo. Choose Enable for Kids to set up a parental lock and then sign in with the account you want to use.

Once setup, you can adjust the hours Alexa is allowed to be in use at different times in the Alexa app under Family & Kids settings.

What should I tell Alexa to do?

When you want Alexa to do a particular task, you can give a command, which can be either long or short.

For example, you can say, "Alexa, turn the volume up on the TV," to make your TV louder.

Or, you can say, "Alexa, show me the weather," or "Alexa,

set a timer for 10 minutes."

To give Alexa a task, click on the Actions icon on the bottom right of the home screen on your Alexa-enabled device. You can then select the appropriate Alexa task from a list of suggestions, or pick a task from the Skills.

What skills can Alexa use?

For example, you can use Alexa for games, check the weather, send messages, find your favorite TV shows and movies, play music, make calls, and control your smart home devices.

How do I use Skills?

When you enable a skill in the Alexa app, you can tell Alexa what you want it to do. For example, say "Alexa, set a timer for five minutes."

Once Alexa has decided what you want to do, you will then hear a chime and the skills will be activated. Alexa will then send the message to the skill that you are using.

Alexa Skills 2: 5 smart skills to try

Thinking of building your own skill? Here are five great skills you can try.

1. Fam Zoo - Offers fun for kids ages 3 and up.

With this skill, kids can listen to, read and react to stories.

Family members can switch back and forth between the stories for a more engaging experience.

2. WunderRational - Provides a fun and entertaining "Guess the Fact" game for kids ages 5 and up.

Three to five questions are asked of the child, and a correct answer will be announced. If the child answers incorrectly, he or she will have to guess what the fact is. If there is still no correct answer, the child gets the prize.

3. The Minimalist - Creates a short piece of music or a sound and transitions the listeners between music.

Listening to this skill will help your child practice music theory.

4. Deep Sleep - Consists of 10 ambient sounds designed to help children fall asleep or stay asleep.

Soothing sounds will also help relax the child.

5. Smart Music - Chooses a song and plays it in a

personalized playlist.

You can choose the age of the child who would like to hear the song.

What are the key features to make Alexa useful?

On the Amazon Echo, you can tell Alexa what you want to do, and then she will follow up and do that for you.

For example, you can say, "Alexa, turn the lights on."

Amazon Echo can also control your smart home devices.

You can say things like, "Alexa, turn the lights on in the living room" or "Alexa, turn the lights off in the kitchen."

Chapter 6 What are the 100+ tips and tricks of Alexa?

1. For Kids:

Set Alexa to a setting so you can listen in but let kids ask simple questions such as how tall you are, what your favorite color is or if you want to go to Grandma's house to play.

2. For the Moms and Dads

If you are reading the morning paper or having coffee in bed, Alexa has a great line-up of podcasts. When you set up the skill, you can choose from different playlists. You can listen to your favorite podcasts like WNYC's On the Media, The New Yorker Radio Hour, etc. for the quick flip between news and current events.

3. Set Alexa to Away Mode for Kids

I often find my kids listening to music in their rooms. In order to send them back to the real world, I tell Alexa to switch to their away mode and they can get back to video games and screens.

4. Set Alexa to get busy mode

When you're trying to get things done, having music on to create a beat and nature sounds for background noise is great. But you need to remember, not everything is music. Sometimes you want your boss to see you at your desk and so, set it to busy mode.

5. Make Alexa repeat.

If you are setting up a timer and she says repeat, set Alexa to a repeating timer to make sure she doesn't stop.

6. Don't be embarrassed.

I do this, and let her read my grocery list back to me.

7. Let Alexa play the news.

Whether you want news headlines or read-only, Alexa has the news.

8. Set Alexa to Alexa Device.

When my kids are having a hard time getting ready, I tell Alexa to set up Alexa Device. It activates all the speakers in the house and lets Alexa tell all the other devices to turn on.

9. Set Alexa to Use In Stores or At Home.

This is great if you have kids and want to know if they are listening at a friend's house. It also makes sense in an office setting to know if people are using the office speakers.

10. Set Alexa to shuffle when she sings.

This is a fun, quick way to play songs with her in a big way.

11. Set Alexa to Speak Different Things.

This is great for book readers.

12. Set Alexa to Custom Home/Ambient for Alexa.

This is really useful for a party. It doesn't matter if you have children, you can still set her up to speak on a loud volume or use the lights in the kitchen.

13. Set Alexa to Adjust to Your Weather.

This is great if you are having company and want to know

if the driveway is slippery before you are going to leave.

14. Tell Alexa to Play a song.

If you are in the kitchen, turn on your Bluetooth and Alexa will play a song.

15. Let Alexa Pick a Song from Your Library.

If you don't like the song, just tell Alexa to pick a new one. If you like a song, she will let you play it over and over again.

16. Make Alexa Say Something New to You Every Day.

17. Set Alexa to Choose a Song from Your Library.

18. When you're cooking in the kitchen, tell Alexa to turn off the light in the kitchen or let her turn on the lights.

19. Set Alexa to If/Then and Then.

20. Turn off all but one fan.

When you're at a dinner party with friends, tell Alexa to turn off the kitchen fan and then tell Alexa that the lights are on.

21. Solve a Rubik's Cube

That's all you need to do. You'll need your Echo device with Alexa, or one with a Bluetooth connection to it. Click here to learn how to play a game using Alexa.

22. Get a ride to the airport

Amazon Prime members, head to Amazon, and click on the Instant Pickup link to get a list of frequently ordered items in your area. Click on your ZIP code, and select the items you want to pick up. Once your items arrive at the shipping center, head to the pickup counter and tell Alexa to confirm.

23. Ask Alexa where Santa is

No need to step outside or watch the news. Alexa will tell you where Santa Claus is on his Christmas Eve delivery routes.

24. Get a haircut at home

Get a haircut at home with a mirror and scissors by using Alexa. Put on a long beard, buy a hat and get on with your life.

25. Add this skill to your home automation setup

This time of year you'll want to consider adding Alexa voice control to your home automation system. You can give it to your home to control connected lights, thermostats, sprinklers, fans, and smart outlets.

26. Make an Instant Pot recipe

Get the recipe for the Instant Pot marinade you are going to need to make your Thanksgiving turkey. To help celebrate the holidays, Amazon has put together some great holiday cooking ideas for you to try. Check out the Instant Pot Center here for more.

27. Favorite books

Use the Echo Spot, Echo Show or Echo Dot to tell Alexa to read you a book and have her read it out loud to you.

28. Watch a 'Bond' movie

After years of telling Alexa you'd watch a 'James Bond' movie to prove you were the coolest girl in school, she's finally listening. Use your Echo device to play 'Bond' films.

29. Catch up on holiday movies

Like Daniel Craig, Amazon's Alexa loves holidays. Use your Echo device to say, "Alexa, tell [movie title]" and listen to the Echo copy the title. She will then stream the appropriate movie and start it playing in the background.

30. Get Alexa to play a TV show

Use your Echo devices to find movies or TV shows to play

on Echo Show, Echo Spot, FireTV Stick or connected Roku device.

31. Alexa read you a story

You can hear one of your favorite stories told by Alexa on your Echo device. Tell her to start the story you want her to tell, and she will start it and you can carry on with your day.

32. Turn on your TV

Echo, Alexa, turn on the TV. This is a great skill for the whole family to share.

33. Ask Alexa who was on SNL

Use your Echo device to ask Alexa who was on Saturday Night Live last week. When the news is on, ask Alexa who's on. She will tell you.

34. Add your phone number to your Alexa

You can easily add your cell number to Alexa. It's a good idea to do it now so you can block any unwanted callers.

35. Give your Amazon Echo device an answer

If you don't know the answer to a question, ask Alexa. She'll tell you.

36. Get Alexa to do the household chores

All you have to do is tell Alexa what you need done, then when you tell her to do it, she will.

37. Tell Alexa how your day is going

When you're busy with your day, tell Alexa how your day is going. She'll tell you and give you updates on your day.

38. Alexa gives you a weather report

You can ask Alexa what the weather is like in your area. If

you're interested in the weather, be sure to follow up with her on how the weather is expected to be over the next few days.

39. Ask Alexa for a sign of what's around you

Use your Echo device to ask Alexa for a sign of what's around you. Alexa will give you a single word or phrase that has a meaning.

40. Take a vacation

Your Alexa will provide you with a list of places to go and people to call if you've given her permission to access your phone contacts.

The list of the bonus 174 tips and tricks of Alexa.

1. "Alexa, update your to-do list" — Find out what's coming up and add to it.
2. "Alexa, enable flashlight on the Echo" — If you have a Philips Hue lightbulb, you can control the light using your Echo.
3. "Alexa, play Rolling Stone on TuneIn" — Alexa will play a podcast from TuneIn, and it looks like your Echo is the center of the party.
4. "Alexa, show me the weather in Orlando" — Alexa will show you the forecast for your location.
5. "Alexa, play songs from Disney Channel" — If you have a Disney Channel soundtracks on your Spotify, your Echo will play it when you ask it to.
6. "Alexa, add it to my favorites" — Alexa will add songs to your library, which is great if you haven't added a song you like to your playlists.
7. "Alexa, control home security system" — You can ask Alexa to control the various security systems you have installed.
8. "Alexa, play audiobooks" — Use a simple voice command to play your favorite audiobooks.
9. "Alexa, play podcasts from Audible" — Alexa will play your favorite Audible book-to-movie or book-to-audio deals.

10. "Alexa, add milk to shopping list" — Add items to your list using Alexa.

11. "Alexa, add Netflix to my favorites" — You can now say you want to watch Netflix with Alexa.

12. "Alexa, how much laundry do I have to do today?" — This works with an Amazon Dash button, Amazon Dash button Plus, and Amazon Dash battery pack.

13. "Alexa, add an app to my favorites" — You can sync all your apps on your Echo with your phone's home screen.

14. "Alexa, add Uber to my home screen" — You can add your ride-hailing service to your home screen and say to Alexa, "Play Uber."

15. "Alexa, play iHeartRadio stations" — Want to listen to music on your Echo? Just ask Alexa, and she'll pull up iHeartRadio on demand stations.

16. "Alexa, enable NPR One" — You can listen to news on NPR's app.

17. "Alexa, stop Spotify music" — Now that Spotify integration with Echo is here, you can stop music playback on your Spotify account.

18. "Alexa, turn off Netflix" — If you want to stop streaming on Netflix you can say "Alexa, pause Netflix" or "Alexa, off Netflix."

19. "Alexa, show me the Cubs scores" — See the latest scores on Chicago's beloved baseball team using your Echo.

20. Advertisement on your local Chicago Cubs baseball team.

21. "Alexa, show me the Wall Street Journal" — You can add the Wall Street Journal app to your Alexa's home screen.

22. "Alexa, turn on CNN" — You can also control CNN from your Echo. Just say, "Alexa, turn on CNN," and Alexa will turn it on and queue it up.

23. "Alexa, go to my calendar" — You can also add your own calendar appointments with Alexa. Just say "Alexa, add a work meeting to my calendar," for example.

24. "Alexa, look up my personal calendar" — If you add your personal calendar to Alexa, you can say, "Alexa, what is my schedule?" and she'll pull up the details of your daily and weekly appointments.

25. "Alexa, look up the weather" — This works with an IFTTT recipe.

26. "Alexa, look up the news of the day" — You can ask Alexa, "Alexa, look me up News of the Day."

27. "Alexa, play audiobooks from Audible" — The rest of your audiobook collection is also available with an Alexa voice command.

28. "Alexa, turn on a lamp" — Just say, "Alexa, turn on the living room lamp," and she'll start lighting your lamp.

29. "Alexa, set an alarm for 7:00 AM" — This is a popular IFTTT recipe that will make your Echo wake up your alarm at 7 AM.

30. "Alexa, read me a book" — You can read Kindle books using an Alexa-enabled device or third-party device, including an Amazon Echo.

31. "Alexa, play books from Audible" — You can play audiobooks using your Echo. Just ask Alexa, "Alexa, play Audible," and she'll pull up your library of audiobooks.

32. "Alexa, turn on a light" — You can turn on your lights using an Alexa device, either by voice, or by ordering a light bulb to your Amazon account.

33. "Alexa, turn on Netflix" — You can also start playing Netflix on your TV with an Echo device. Say "Alexa, play Netflix" and she'll turn on your TV.

34. "Alexa, turn off the bedroom lights" — You can turn off your lights by using your Echo devices. Just say, "Alexa, turn off the bedroom lights," and she'll shut off the lights.

35. "Alexa, read me my email" — You can also use your Echo devices to read your emails to you. Say, "Alexa, read me my email" and she'll bring up your messages in Gmail.

36. "Alexa, find my phone" — You can ask Alexa to find your smartphone by just saying, "Alexa, find my phone," and she'll open up the Find My iPhone app on your iOS or Android device.

37. "Alexa, turn on the TV" — You can turn on your TV with an Echo device, like the Amazon Fire TV, or an Apple TV, or whatever media streamer you prefer. Just say, "Alexa, turn on the TV," and she'll control the TV with an Alexa device.

38. "Alexa, turn on the bedroom light" — You can use your Alexa devices to turn on your bedroom lights. Just say, "Alexa, turn on the bedroom light" and she'll turn on the lights in your bedroom.

39. "Alexa, turn on the bathroom light" — You can also use your Alexa devices to turn on your bathroom light. Just say, "Alexa, turn on the bathroom light," and she'll turn the light on.

40. "Alexa, play music for a party" — You can use your Echo devices to play your favorite music during a party. Just say, "Alexa, play party music," and she'll start playing music for your party.

41. "Alexa, tell me a joke" — You can play a joke with Alexa. Just say, "Alexa, tell me a joke," and she'll tell a joke.

42. "Alexa, say something romantic" — You can play a romantic song with Alexa. Just say, "Alexa, play a romantic song," and she'll play a romantic song.

43. "Alexa, remind me to take my medications" — You can also use your Alexa devices to remind you to take your medications, including insulin, vitamins, and other medications. Just say, "Alexa, remind me

to take my medications," and she'll bring up your medication list.

44. "Alexa, set a sleep timer" — You can also set a sleep timer on your Echo devices. Just say, "Alexa, set a sleep timer," and she'll automatically turn off your device after a set amount of time has passed.

45. "Alexa, turn on the bedroom light" — You can also use your Alexa devices to turn on your bedroom lights. Just say, "Alexa, turn on the bedroom light," and she'll turn on the light in your bedroom.

46. "Alexa, turn off the TV" — You can also use your Alexa devices to turn off your TV. Just say, "Alexa, turn off the TV," and she'll turn the TV off.

47. "Alexa, play a comedy" — You can also play a comedy with Alexa. Just say, "Alexa, play a comedy," and she'll start playing a comedy on your Echo device.

48. "Alexa, repeat that" — You can also use your Alexa devices to repeat what you say. Just say, "Alexa, repeat that," and she'll replay what you said in the same way you said it.

49. "Alexa, set a timer for 20 minutes" — You can also use your Alexa devices to set a timer for 20 minutes. Say, "Alexa, set a timer for 20 minutes," and she'll start counting down the time.

50. "Alexa, stop saying 'Hey' every time you say something" — You can also try a different

command. Just say, "Alexa, stop saying 'Hey' every time you say something."

51. "Alexa, skip this song" — You can also use your Alexa devices to skip a song you're playing, by saying, "Alexa, skip this song."

52. "Alexa, turn up the music" — You can also use your Alexa devices to adjust your music by using Alexa. Just say, "Alexa, turn up the music," and she'll adjust your music to the volume you want it at.

53. "Alexa, rewind it" — You can also use your Alexa devices to rewind a TV show or movie you've started watching, by saying, "Alexa, rewind it."

54. "Alexa, set a new volume" — You can also use your Alexa devices to adjust your music by using Alexa. Say, "Alexa, set a new volume," and she'll adjust the volume on your device.

55. "Alexa, start next episode" — You can also use your Alexa devices to pause what you're watching, by saying, "Alexa, start next episode."

56. "Alexa, resume from last episode" — You can also use your Alexa devices to resume watching where you left off, by saying, "Alexa, resume from last episode."

57. "Alexa, change the volume" — You can also use your Alexa devices to adjust the volume on your device. Just say, "Alexa, change the volume," and she'll change the volume on your device.

58. "Alexa, lower the volume" — You can also use your Alexa devices to lower the volume on your device. Just say, "Alexa, lower the volume," and she'll lower the volume on your device.

59. "Alexa, turn off the TV" — You can also use your Alexa devices to turn off the TV. Just say, "Alexa, turn off the TV," and she'll turn off your device.

60. "Alexa, turn off the bedroom light" — You can also use your Alexa devices to turn off the bedroom light. Just say, "Alexa, turn off the bedroom light," and she'll turn on the light in your bedroom.

61. "Alexa, play a comedy" — You can also use your Alexa devices to play a comedy. Just say, "Alexa, play a comedy," and she'll start playing a comedy on your Echo device.

62. "Alexa, play 'You're the Man' by Bruno Mars" — You can also use your Alexa devices to play a comedy. Just say, "Alexa, play 'You're the Man' by Bruno Mars," and she'll start playing a comedy on your Echo device.

63. "Alexa, mute this song" — You can also use your Alexa devices to mute a song, by saying, "Alexa, mute this song."

64. "Alexa, stop listening" — You can also use your Alexa devices to stop listening, by saying, "Alexa, stop listening."

65. "Alexa, play 'Raindrops Keep Fallin' on my Head'" — You can also use your Alexa devices to play a

comedy. Just say, "Alexa, play 'Raindrops Keep Fallin' on my Head'" and she'll start playing a comedy on your Echo device.

66. "Alexa, play 'Casablanca' by Gene Kelly" — You can also use your Alexa devices to play a comedy. Just say, "Alexa, play 'Casablanca' by Gene Kelly," and she'll start playing a comedy on your Echo device.

67. "Alexa, turn up the volume" — You can also use your Alexa devices to increase the volume on your device. Just say, "Alexa, turn up the volume," and she'll increase the volume on your device.

68. "Alexa, pause this song" — You can also use your Alexa devices to pause a song. Just say, "Alexa, pause this song," and she'll pause the song.

69. "Alexa, resume playing" — You can also use your Alexa devices to resume playing a song. Just say, "Alexa, resume playing," and she'll resume playing the song on your Echo device.

70. "Alexa, play this song" — You can also use your Alexa devices to play a song. Just say, "Alexa, play this song," and she'll start playing a song on your device.

71. "Alexa, play a comedy" — You can also use your Alexa devices to play a comedy. Just say, "Alexa, play a comedy," and she'll start playing a comedy on your device.

72. "Alexa, play a Disney movie" — You can also use your Alexa devices to play a Disney movie. Just say,

"Alexa, play a Disney movie," and she'll start playing a Disney movie on your device.

73. "Alexa, play TV shows" — You can also use your Alexa devices to play a TV show. Just say, "Alexa, play TV shows," and she'll start playing a TV show on your device.

74. "Alexa, play music" — You can also use your Alexa devices to play music. Just say, "Alexa, play music," and she'll start playing a song on your device.

75. "Alexa, what song is this?" — You can also use your Alexa devices to play a song on your device. Just say, "Alexa, what song is this?" to play a song on your device.

76. "Alexa, play this" — You can also use your Alexa devices to play a song on your device. Just say, "Alexa, play this," and she'll start playing a song on your device.

77. "Alexa, who is this?" — You can also use your Alexa devices to play a song on your device. Just say, "Alexa, who is this?" to play a song on your device.

78. "Alexa, play this audio" — You can also use your Alexa devices to play music. Just say, "Alexa, play this audio," and she'll start playing a song on your device.

79. "Alexa, this song" — You can also use your Alexa devices to play a song on your device. Just say, "Alexa, play this song," and she'll start playing a song on your device.

80. "Alexa, start this podcast" — You can also use your Alexa devices to play a podcast. Just say, "Alexa, start this podcast," and she'll start playing a podcast on your device.

81. "Alexa, start this podcast in Spanish" — You can also use your Alexa devices to play a podcast in Spanish. Just say, "Alexa, start this podcast in Spanish," and she'll start playing a podcast in Spanish on your device.

82. "Alexa, skip this song" — You can also use your Alexa devices to skip a song on your device. Just say, "Alexa, skip this song," and she'll skip to the next song on your device.

83. "Alexa, pause" — You can also use your Alexa devices to pause a song on your device. Just say, "Alexa, pause," and she'll pause your song on your device.

84. "Alexa, stop playing this song" — You can also use your Alexa devices to stop playing a song on your device. Just say, "Alexa, stop playing this song," and she'll stop playing your song on your device.

85. "Alexa, show me something funny" — You can also use your Alexa devices to search for something funny. Just say, "Alexa, show me something funny," and she'll show you something funny on your device.

86. "Alexa, turn this up" — You can also use your Alexa devices to control your music. Just say, "Alexa, turn

this up," and she'll increase your volume on your device.

87. "Alexa, turn the volume down" — You can also use your Alexa devices to control your music. Just say, "Alexa, turn the volume down," and she'll decrease your volume on your device.

88. "Alexa, next song" — You can also use your Alexa devices to play a song on your device. Just say, "Alexa, play a song," and she'll play a song on your device.

89. "Alexa, stop playing" — You can also use your Alexa devices to stop playing a song on your device. Just say, "Alexa, stop playing," and she'll stop playing your song on your device.

90. "Alexa, volume down" — You can also use your Alexa devices to adjust the volume on your device. Just say, "Alexa, volume down," and she'll adjust your volume on your device.

91. "Alexa, get me something to read" — You can also use your Alexa devices to read a book to you. Just say, "Alexa, get me something to read," and she'll tell you a story on your device.

92. "Alexa, tell me a story" — You can also use your Alexa devices to tell you a story. Just say, "Alexa, tell me a story," and she'll read a story on your device.

93. "Alexa, add this song" — You can also use your Alexa devices to add a song to your collection. Just

say, "Alexa, add this song," and she'll add it to your collection.

94. "Alexa, add this song to a playlist" — You can also use your Alexa devices to add a song to a playlist. Just say, "Alexa, add this song to a playlist," and she'll add the song to your playlist.

95. "Alexa, ask me a question" — You can also use your Alexa devices to ask a question. Just say, "Alexa, ask me a question," and she'll respond to you.

96. "Alexa, ask Jay Leno a question" — You can also use your Alexa devices to ask a question to Jay Leno. Just say, "Alexa, ask Jay Leno a question," and he'll respond to you.

97. "Alexa, play National Geographic " — You can also use your Alexa devices to play National Geographic shows. Just say, "Alexa, play National Geographic," and she'll start playing a National Geographic show on your device.

98. "Alexa, play CNN" — You can also use your Alexa devices to play CNN shows. Just say, "Alexa, play CNN," and she'll play a CNN show on your device.

99. "Alexa, turn on the TV" — You can also use your Alexa devices to turn on the TV. Just say, "Alexa, turn on the TV," and she'll turn on your TV.

100. "Alexa, switch to BBC World News" — You can also use your Alexa devices to switch to the BBC World News channel. Just say, "Alexa, switch to

BBC World News," and she'll switch to the BBC World News channel.

101. "Alexa, go to sleep" — You can also use your Alexa devices to tell Alexa to go to sleep. Just say, "Alexa, go to sleep," and she'll turn off your devices and head for bed.

102. "Alexa, ask Jamie Oliver a cooking question" — You can also use your Alexa devices to ask a cooking question to Jamie Oliver. Just say, "Alexa, ask Jamie Oliver a cooking question," and she'll give you advice.

103. "Alexa, switch to Sling TV" — You can also use your Alexa devices to switch to Sling TV. Just say, "Alexa, switch to Sling TV," and she'll switch to the Sling TV channel you selected in the previous step.

104. "Alexa, play NPR" — You can also use your Alexa devices to play NPR news. Just say, "Alexa, play NPR," and she'll play a NPR news show on your device.

105. "Alexa, start a Flash Briefing" — You can also use your Alexa devices to play a Flash Briefing. Just say, "Alexa, start a Flash Briefing," and she'll play a Flash Briefing on your device.

106. "Alexa, change my alarm tone" — You can also use your Alexa devices to change your alarm tone. Just say, "Alexa, change my alarm tone," and she'll change your alarm tone to another song.

107. "Alexa, tell me the news" — You can also use your Alexa devices to get news. Just say, "Alexa, tell me the news," and she'll tell you what's going on in the news.

108. "Alexa, tell me a joke" — You can also use your Alexa devices to tell you a joke. Just say, "Alexa, tell me a joke," and she'll give you a joke.

109. "Alexa, play a comedy podcast" — You can also use your Alexa devices to listen to a comedy podcast. Just say, "Alexa, play a comedy podcast," and she'll play a comedy podcast on your device.

110. "Alexa, tell me a joke" — You can also use your Alexa devices to tell you a joke. Just say, "Alexa, tell me a joke," and she'll tell you a joke.

111. "Alexa, change the channel" — You can also use your Alexa devices to change the channel. Just say, "Alexa, change the channel," and she'll change your device's channel.

112. "Alexa, skip ahead 30 seconds" — You can also use your Alexa devices to skip ahead 30 seconds to a show. Just say, "Alexa, skip ahead 30 seconds," and she'll do it.

113. "Alexa, show me CES coverage" — You can also use your Alexa devices to see CES coverage on your device. Just say, "Alexa, show me CES coverage," and she'll find a CES coverage for you.

114. "Alexa, find me a recipe" — You can also use your Alexa devices to find recipes on Pinterest. Just say,

"Alexa, find me a recipe," and she'll ask you what you want.

115. "Alexa, show me sports highlights" — You can also use your Alexa devices to watch sports on television. Just say, "Alexa, show me sports highlights," and she'll show you highlights from your favorite sporting events on television.

116. "Alexa, show me Wall Street Journal" — You can also use your Alexa devices to watch Wall Street Journal news coverage. Just say, "Alexa, show me Wall Street Journal," and she'll play news headlines on your device.

117. "Alexa, show me 'SNL' on Hulu" — You can also use your Alexa devices to watch SNL on Hulu. Just say, "Alexa, show me 'SNL'" and she'll do it.

118. "Alexa, help me order takeaway" — You can also use your Alexa devices to order takeaway. Just say, "Alexa, help me order takeaway," and she'll give you a few options.

119. "Alexa, set an alarm" — You can also use your Alexa devices to set an alarm. Just say, "Alexa, set an alarm," and she'll do it.

120. "Alexa, turn off the TV" — You can also use your Alexa devices to turn off the TV. Just say, "Alexa, turn off the TV," and she'll turn the TV off.

121. "Alexa, lock the door" — You can also use your Alexa devices to lock the door. Just say, "Alexa, lock the door," and she'll lock the door.

122. "Alexa, play a podcast" — You can also use your Alexa devices to listen to a podcast. Just say, "Alexa, play a podcast," and she'll play a podcast.

123. "Alexa, set a timer" — You can also use your Alexa devices to set a timer. Just say, "Alexa, set a timer," and she'll set a timer for you.

124. "Alexa, play a trivia game" — You can also use your Alexa devices to play a trivia game. Just say, "Alexa, play a trivia game," and she'll play a trivia game for you.

125. "Alexa, play a news round-up" — You can also use your Alexa devices to play a news round-up. Just say, "Alexa, play a news round-up," and she'll play a round-up of the news.

126. "Alexa, set a timer for 10 minutes" — You can also use your Alexa devices to set a timer. Just say, "Alexa, set a timer for 10 minutes," and she'll set a timer for 10 minutes.

127. "Alexa, take a selfie" — You can also use your Alexa devices to take selfies. Just say, "Alexa, take a selfie," and she'll take a selfie with you.

128. "Alexa, stop the music" — You can also use your Alexa devices to stop the music. Just say, "Alexa, stop the music," and she'll stop the music.

129. "Alexa, stop recording" — You can also use your Alexa devices to stop the camera from recording. Just say, "Alexa, stop recording," and she'll stop the camera from recording.

130. "Alexa, play an audiobook" — You can also use your Alexa devices to play audiobooks. Just say, "Alexa, play an audiobook," and she'll play a book.

131. "Alexa, turn down the temperature" — You can also use your Alexa devices to set the temperature. Just say, "Alexa, turn down the temperature," and she'll set the temperature.

132. "Alexa, make a pizza" — You can also use your Alexa devices to make a pizza. Just say, "Alexa, make a pizza," and she'll cook you a pizza.

133. "Alexa, add milk" — You can also use your Alexa devices to add milk. Just say, "Alexa, add milk," and she'll add milk.

134. "Alexa, change the music" — You can also use your Alexa devices to change the music. Just say, "Alexa, change the music," and she'll change the music.

135. "Alexa, put it in the toaster" — You can also use your Alexa devices to put the toast in the toaster. Just say, "Alexa, put it in the toaster," and she'll put the toast in the toaster.

136. "Alexa, start the dishwasher" — You can also use your Alexa devices to start the dishwasher. Just say, "Alexa, start the dishwasher," and she'll start the dishwasher.

137. "Alexa, remove the trash" — You can also use your Alexa devices to remove the trash. Just say, "Alexa, remove the trash," and she'll remove the trash.

138. "Alexa, empty the dishwasher" — You can also use your Alexa devices to empty the dishwasher. Just say, "Alexa, empty the dishwasher," and she'll empty the dishwasher.

139. "Alexa, make a phone call" — You can also use your Alexa devices to make a phone call. Just say, "Alexa, make a phone call," and she'll call a number for you.

140. "Alexa, remind me to take out the trash" — You can also use your Alexa devices to remind you to take out the trash. Just say, "Alexa, remind me to take out the trash," and she'll remind you to take out the trash.

141. "Alexa, show me the front door" — You can also use your Alexa devices to show you the front door. Just say, "Alexa, show me the front door," and she'll show you the front door.

142. "Alexa, where's my car" — You can also use your Alexa devices to show you where your car is. Just say, "Alexa, where's my car?" and she'll tell you where it is.

143. "Alexa, close the garage door" — You can also use your Alexa devices to close the garage door. Just say, "Alexa, close the garage door," and she'll close the garage door.

144. "Alexa, turn the lights off" — You can also use your Alexa devices to turn the lights off. Just say,

"Alexa, turn the lights off," and she'll turn the lights off.

145. "Alexa, turn on the bedroom light" — You can also use your Alexa devices to turn on the bedroom light. Just say, "Alexa, turn on the bedroom light," and she'll turn on the bedroom light.

146. "Alexa, good night" — You can also use your Alexa devices to turn on the bedroom lights and to turn off the bedroom lights. Just say, "Alexa, good night," and she'll turn the lights on and off.

147. "Alexa, turn on the fan" — You can also use your Alexa devices to turn on the fan. Just say, "Alexa, turn on the fan," and she'll turn on the fan.

148. "Alexa, dim the living room lights" — You can also use your Alexa devices to dim the living room lights. Just say, "Alexa, dim the living room lights," and she'll dim the lights.

149. "Alexa, set an alarm for a specific time" — You can also use your Alexa devices to set a specific time for an alarm. Just say, "Alexa, set a specific alarm time," and she'll set a time.

150. "Alexa, open the smart light" — You can also use your Alexa devices to open the smart light. Just say, "Alexa, open the smart light," and she'll open the smart light.

151. "Alexa, turn on the living room lamp" — You can also use your Alexa devices to turn on the living

room lamp. Just say, "Alexa, turn on the living room lamp," and she'll turn the lamp on.

152. "Alexa, turn off the living room lamp" — You can also use your Alexa devices to turn off the living room lamp. Just say, "Alexa, turn off the living room lamp," and she'll turn the lamp off.

153. "Alexa, open the smart bulb" — You can also use your Alexa devices to open the smart bulb. Just say, "Alexa, open the smart bulb," and she'll open the smart bulb.

154. "Alexa, turn on the bedroom lamp" — You can also use your Alexa devices to turn on the bedroom lamp. Just say, "Alexa, turn on the bedroom lamp," and she'll turn the lamp on.

155. "Alexa, close the smart light" — You can also use your Alexa devices to close the smart light. Just say, "Alexa, close the smart light," and she'll close the smart light.

156. "Alexa, put on a night light" — You can also use your Alexa devices to set a specific time for an alarm. Just say, "Alexa, put on a specific alarm time," and she'll set a specific alarm time.

157. "Alexa, do you want to talk about it?" — You can also use your Alexa devices to set a specific time for an alarm. Just say, "Alexa, do you want to talk about it?" She'll answer your questions.

158. "Alexa, set an alarm for a specific time" — You can also use your Alexa devices to set a specific alarm.

Just say, "Alexa, set a specific alarm time," and she'll set a specific alarm.

159. "Alexa, close the shades" — You can also use your Alexa devices to close the shades. Just say, "Alexa, close the shades," and she'll close the shades.

160. "Alexa, turn off the lights" — You can also use your Alexa devices to turn off the lights. Just say, "Alexa, turn off the lights," and she'll turn the lights off.

161. "Alexa, ask light what time it is" — You can also use your Alexa devices to ask a light what time it is. Just say, "Alexa, ask light what time it is," and she'll reply.

162. "Alexa, open the door" — You can also use your Alexa devices to open the door. Just say, "Alexa, open the door," and she'll open the door.

163. "Alexa, light up the living room" — You can also use your Alexa devices to light up the living room. Just say, "Alexa, light up the living room," and she'll turn on the lights.

164. "Alexa, turn the TV off" — You can also use your Alexa devices to turn off the TV. Just say, "Alexa, turn off the TV," and she'll turn the TV off.

165. "Alexa, start a movie" — You can also use your Alexa devices to start a movie. Just say, "Alexa, start a movie," and she'll start a movie.

166. "Alexa, turn the kitchen light on" — You can also use your Alexa devices to turn on the kitchen light.

Just say, "Alexa, turn on the kitchen light," and she'll turn on the light.

167. "Alexa, turn on the kitchen light off" — You can also use your Alexa devices to turn off the kitchen light. Just say, "Alexa, turn on the kitchen light off," and she'll turn the light off.

168. "Alexa, open the garage" — You can also use your Alexa devices to open the garage door. Just say, "Alexa, open the garage," and she'll open the garage door.

169. "Alexa, close the door" — You can also use your Alexa devices to close the door. Just say, "Alexa, close the door," and she'll close the door.

170. "Alexa, ask Echo where I left my car" — You can also use your Alexa devices to ask a car to remember where you left it. Just say, "Alexa, ask Echo where I left my car," and she'll tell you where you left your car.

171. "Alexa, ask Echo to lock my door" — You can also use your Alexa devices to lock your door. Just say, "Alexa, ask Echo to lock my door," and she'll lock the door.

172. "Alexa, ask Echo to unlock my door" — You can also use your Alexa devices to unlock your door. Just say, "Alexa, ask Echo to unlock my door," and she'll unlock the door.

173. "Alexa, ask Echo to open my garage" — You can also use your Alexa devices to open your garage

door. Just say, "Alexa, ask Echo to open my garage," and she'll open your garage door.

174. "Alexa, ask Echo to close my curtains" — You can also use your Alexa devices to close your curtains. Just say, "Alexa, ask Echo to close my curtains," and she'll close your curtains.

Chapter 7 What facts about Amazon Echo devices?

The smart speaker was introduced by Amazon in November, with the voice-activated Alexa available as a feature. Unlike its Google Home and Apple HomePod rivals, Alexa is able to answer general knowledge questions, music requests and execute the occasional task. A smaller Dot smart speaker was added in November, with a high-end Echo device following in the autumn of the same year.

The Amazon Echo is capable of answering questions, streaming music and streaming podcasts, with dozens of third-party skills available, although only Echo devices that have been linked to the Echo Connect speaker dock can connect with an external speaker system. The Dot has been joined by the cheaper Echo Dot Kids Edition speaker. The new Echo Plus speaker was unveiled in October, along with an Echo Spot, as well as a reworked Echo Show device.

The Echo Spot is a smart alarm clock and smart speaker

hybrid that will appear in later 2017, while the Echo Plus has its own smart home hub capability, providing built-in smart home functions and compatibility with Alexa-powered SmartThings home automation hubs. The Echo Plus can also be used as an external alarm clock. Amazon also announced a new Echo Input speaker on the same day as the new Echo Plus model.

Alexa-powered smart cameras are available from a range of manufacturers, including Amazon, at the time of writing, such as the DropCam Flex 2 and the iRobot Roomba 960. A Smart Camera system from Logitech was also launched, along with a Google Home Hub.

Alexa-powered virtual personal assistants are also available from some manufacturers, such as the Amazon Echo Show and Amazon Echo Spot. Amazon has a broad range of headphones, with a new generation of Bluetooth wireless headphones, the Dash Wireless Bluetooth Earbuds.

The new Bluetooth speaker from Libratone is available from 15 October, while the JBL Link 300 is Amazon Alexa-compatible and available from Amazon at a discounted price.

Alexa-powered smart home hub systems

The Amazon Echo Spot is Amazon's Echo-powered smart camera that can connect to any regular Echo device via the Alexa app. The Echo Spot, Amazon's first video-enabled smart camera, has a 2.5-inch display and can be used for video calls, with a seven-megapixel camera and an infrared LED to support vision for night vision.

The Echo Spot can connect to other smart devices via the Smart Home Skills API. A range of products are compatible, including lighting, smart plugs, motion sensors and security cameras. The Echo Spot is available in the UK from 12 December, with a cheaper, smaller version, the Echo Spot Mini, released on 6 November. The Echo Spot Mini will also be coming to the US, Canada and Germany.

The Amazon Echo Input is an alternative to the Echo Dot for control of existing smart home lighting systems. The device is compatible with smart light bulbs, dimmers and switches from manufacturers including Honeywell, Philips Hue, WeMo, TP-Link and Lutron. It was revealed in

October, with the smaller Echo Input launched in November.

The Echo Input replaces a conventional wireless speaker and plays music via Wi-Fi or Bluetooth. Like the Echo Dot, it uses Amazon's Alexa voice assistant to respond to voice commands. It is also compatible with Amazon Music, Prime Music, Deezer, Pandora, iHeartRadio, TuneIn and other music streaming services.

The Echo Link is an alternative to the Echo Link Amp, which is available in the UK. The Link is an Amazon Echo-branded speaker that can be linked with other audio equipment to expand its functionality. It can be used to stream from music services such as Amazon Music, as well as from physical hi-fi equipment such as consoles, in-ear and wireless headphones. The Link will be available from 11 December, with pre-orders being taken from 11 December.

Echo Link Amp and Echo Input are both available in the US, but US customers have the option of choosing between a black and white version of either.

The Amazon Echo Sub is a more traditional Echo speaker that connects to existing speakers via 3.5mm. It can be used for playing music when there's no other Echo speakers around. The speaker connects via Bluetooth to a phone or an external audio device such as an Amazon Fire TV Stick 4K or Sonos speakers. The Amazon Echo Sub is available in the US from 3 December, with pre-orders being taken from 15 October.

Amazon Music service

Amazon Music is available in the UK via a range of Echo devices, with a new Echo Input and Amazon Echo Sub making the service a multiroom system. Spotify is also available in the UK and available via the Alexa Skills Kit.

Echo Auto

The Echo Auto is Amazon's take on the connected car, allowing owners to play music, manage traffic and get news headlines hands-free. As it is powered by Alexa, you can control it with voice commands, and Amazon has added in the ability to place calls and control smart home devices.

Amazon Alexa is the cloud-based voice service that powers the Echo devices, and you can use it to control your smart home devices using only your voice. It is also the system that responds to voice commands on the Echo devices, which come with a camera to enable users to make video calls to other Echo owners.

Echo Plus (2nd generation)

The second generation Echo Plus is Amazon's best-selling device in the Echo range, featuring enhanced stereo sound, a nicer design and improved audio performance. It was released in the UK in October, and the US.

It features eight microphones so you can pick up your

voice from across the room, and it comes with a wall plug and a USB port to connect additional devices. It comes with a Philips Hue smart bulb that can be controlled with voice commands. It also integrates well with other smart devices around the home, for example, you can change the heating using the Echo Plus.

The Echo Plus is also the only device with a Zigbee smart home hub built in. Zigbee is a communications protocol that supports other smart home devices and has more than 60% of the smart home market share, making it the ideal choice for smart lighting and smart home security systems.

Echo Plus is Alexa's most compact smart home device, featuring a new soft-color charcoal fabric. The top of the device has the volume and mute buttons, as well as a three-way button used to access the various Alexa features. It has a four-microphone array, which Amazon claims will pick up your voice from across the room and is always listening to give you full and accurate responses.

Amazon Echo Show (2nd generation)

The Echo Show is an updated version of the original Echo Show, which arrived on the market. It has a 10.1-inch display that can be used for watching video, reading the news and, thanks to Amazon's smart video camera, can be used to make video calls.

You can also stream video from your phone to the Echo Show using Amazon's native video service, Prime Video, which is available in the UK and will soon be available in the US. You can't use the Echo Show to watch YouTube videos, though, and YouTube support for the device has been cut off as of October.

There's also an 8-megapixel camera on the front of the device, with an LED flash that's used to provide more accurate picture quality. There's an 8-microphone array on the device to provide clear audio, and the device can also be used to make video calls via the Amazon Alexa app.

The Echo Show has a down-firing speaker, while the base has an active bass radiator to help improve sound quality when playing music or using the various Echo voice-control features.

Echo Sub (2nd generation)

You may not have heard of the Echo Sub, but Amazon plans to release it in the UK and US before Christmas.

Amazon says the Echo Sub can convert existing Echo speakers into full stereo systems without having to add an additional device. If you have an Amazon Echo Plus, Echo, Echo Dot or Echo Show, you can connect the Echo Sub via Bluetooth or an auxiliary cable to create a second wireless audio system in your home.

You can also use the Echo Sub as a Bluetooth speaker, and

the device has a 3.5mm aux jack, so you can use it to connect it to non-Echo devices as well. The Echo Sub can be used to play music through two Echo speakers

Amazon Smart Plug (2nd generation)

In the US, the Amazon Smart Plug is a new product that allows you to control and schedule lights, appliances, and other smart home devices using the Alexa app on your smartphone, or the Alexa voice assistant.

To use the Amazon Smart Plug you'll need an Amazon Echo smart speaker (either the original Amazon Echo or Amazon Echo Plus). To use the Smart Plug, you must be an Amazon Prime member.

Amazon Echo Input (2nd gen)

The Echo Input is a £25 smart speaker for people who

don't already own an Amazon Echo speaker. The Echo Input can be placed on a nightstand or desk, and it's designed to act as the centrepiece for a Sonos-like home audio setup that's been customised to play music from Amazon's music streaming service.

Amazon says the Echo Input can pair with any existing Bluetooth speaker and will wirelessly stream audio to it, and you can ask Alexa to play music on the Echo Input using the same voice-control capabilities you're used to using with an Echo speaker.

The Echo Input is an upcoming speaker that can pair with other Bluetooth speakers

The Echo Link Amp and Link South

The Echo Link Amp and Link South are two additional wireless audio devices Amazon is introducing alongside the new Echo devices.

The Echo Link Amp is a device that can wirelessly stream music from an Echo device or other Bluetooth devices, and also have Alexa voice controls integrated. The Echo Link Amp also has an output power of 500 watts, meaning it can play music at a full home stereo system level.

The Link South is a smaller, more portable wireless speaker, with Amazon promising it will have 360-degree sound. It has a 2-inch fabric mesh fabric dome with acoustic panels to absorb energy and ensure high sound quality. Like the Echo Link Amp, the Link South will have Alexa voice controls integrated, but Amazon says it will allow listeners to connect with their phone instead of using an Echo device to control the music.

The Echo Input is a speaker that can wirelessly pair with other Bluetooth speakers

Smart light switch

The Echo Wall Switch is a smart light switch for the wall

that can control up to 100 Alexa devices. The light switch can be placed anywhere in the home, and you can make changes to its brightness, as well as set schedules so that it turns on and off at particular times.

Smart Socket

The Smart Socket is a USB adapter that you plug into the wall to plug in accessories, such as external hard drives or other USB devices. It supports two 5V ports, so you can plug in additional devices if you have multiple USB chargers around your house.

AmazonBasics Microwave

AmazonBasics Microwave is a smart microwave oven that can support different voice assistants. The smart microwave oven can also play music, watch videos and answer simple questions, and you can get a recipe from Alexa right when you start cooking.

Fire TV Recast

The Fire TV Recast is a DVR box that wirelessly streams live and recorded television shows to your Echo Show, Echo Spot or Fire TV. The Recast can record all of the live programming from over-the-air broadcasts.

The Recast can also record the previous seven days of programming, and you can use Alexa to start or stop recordings as well as to search for shows.

Connected soundbar

The Dolby Atmos Wireless Audio Receiver is a multi-room

wireless soundbar that supports Dolby Atmos, DTS:X and Dolby Vision.

The Dolby Atmos Wireless Audio Receiver connects to two receivers in a multi-room setup and can wirelessly play up to seven different music tracks. This soundbar is designed to make up for the lack of Atmos support on Amazon Echo devices, but the company has said that a future update will enable this speaker to support the immersive audio format.

Ring Video Doorbell Pro

The Ring Video Doorbell Pro is a smart video doorbell that connects with Alexa and your smartphone via an app to let you see who is at your front door and what they are wearing.

It can also record and save up to 30 seconds of video prior to and after it senses someone is at your door, and it works with other Ring smart home devices including smart locks, garage door openers and solar panels.

The Ring Video Doorbell Pro is available for pre-order in the US starting in November.

Ring Alarm

Ring Alarm is a smart security system with live monitoring that you can manage using your smartphone.

Ring Alarm is a smart security system with live monitoring that you can manage using your smartphone

You can monitor and adjust your security cameras and door locks, as well as contact emergency services if you need to, with a single keypad. The Ring Alarm starter kit includes a keypad, motion sensor, contact sensor and a key fob.

Ring Spotlight Cam

The Ring Spotlight Cam is a smart outdoor security camera that you can connect to your smart speaker to see and speak with people at your door.

Ring Spotlight Cam is a smart outdoor security camera that you can connect to your smart speaker to see and speak with people at your door

The Spotlight Cam has two-way audio and allows you to see people approaching and hiding in your yard, as well as zoom in and highlight people who have your smart speaker linked to them.

Ring Video Doorbell 2

The Ring Video Doorbell 2 is a smart doorbell that you can connect to your smart speaker so that you can see and speak with people at your door.

Ring Video Doorbell 2 is a smart doorbell that you can connect to your smart speaker so that you can see and speak with people at your door

The Doorbell 2 also uses audio-visual tones that help you differentiate between visitors and other sounds, and you can customize the ringtones that play when you are away from home.

Ring Stick Up Cam

The Ring Stick Up Cam is a smart security camera that uses a variety of motion detection and person detection features to keep an eye on your front door and outdoor area.

The Stick Up Cam also works with your Ring smart

speaker, and you can view live video and alerts on your phone or tablet.

Ring Spotlight Cam 2

The Ring Spotlight Cam 2 is a smart outdoor security camera that you can connect to your smart speaker so that you can see and speak with people at your door.

The Spotlight Cam 2 also works with your Ring smart speaker, and you can view live video and alerts on your phone or tablet.

Gadgets for Alexa's world

Amazon has a host of new and updated devices available for Alexa devices, including new tools for Amazon Alexa users in the UK.

The launch of the Echo Input comes as Amazon launches the Alexa-enabled smart speaker

Amazon Echo Input

The Echo Input is a small dongle that plugs into your existing speaker to give Alexa hands-free control over music and play music stored on a flash drive or Fire TV Stick.

You can pre-order the Echo Input now.

The Echo Sub is the latest in a long line of wireless speaker devices from Amazon

Echo Sub

The Echo Sub is the latest in a long line of wireless speaker devices from Amazon, and it's intended to add a sub-bass boost to the bottom of a surround sound system.

There's also an updated Echo Plus speaker that can be used for a smart home hub and video doorbell.

Amazon Echo Wall Clock

The Echo Wall Clock is the first gadget to use Alexa as a hub for your smart home devices.

An updated version of the Amazon Echo Show has a smaller 10-inch HD display

New Amazon Echo Show

The Echo Show is the latest smart screen device from Amazon, and it now comes with a 10-inch HD display and improved sound.

It also features better-quality speakers and a full selection of Skills from the Amazon Echo range.

New Amazon Smart Plug

Amazon is rolling out a new line of smart plug devices that are equipped with Alexa.

They can be plugged into any power outlet and the Alexa software will determine how much power is being used at a given time and when it needs to be used.

Amazon Key

Amazon Key is a new service that allows Amazon delivery workers to put packages inside a customer's house, provided the customer is an Amazon Prime member and lets the delivery workers into their house using a smart lock and security camera.

When the Amazon delivery person arrives, a door buzzer will go off and they will be given a one-time code to enter. The delivery person will be prompted to find your package and seal it safely before leaving.

The system is currently only available in select areas in the US.

Consumer Radio Stick

The Amazon Cloud Cam and Echo Show can play audio from a connected computer

Amazon is rolling out the Radio Stick, a device that connects to a Chromecast or Apple TV to allow Amazon's Echo devices to play audio and video from a connected computer.

Amazon Screensaver

You can also set up a Wall Clock and a desktop wallpaper on an Echo Show and make the screen go dark at certain times

Amazon Dash

Dash will let you order a product without having to leave

your seat and talk to a live person

Dash is a service that allows you to order a product without having to leave your seat and talk to a live person.

With Dash you can order food, household items or even alcohol.

You can use Amazon Dash to add products to a grocery cart, or reorder paper towels.

Amazon's first smart speaker, the Amazon Echo

Alongside its Echo speakers, Amazon has unveiled the Echo, its first smart speaker.

The Amazon Echo is designed to turn the Echo into a more capable smart speaker, with better audio quality and the ability to control smart home gadgets.

It can play music, access your online shopping basket, check the weather, give you an answer to any question, read audiobooks out loud and, much like the original Echo, be used to play games.

The Amazon Echo is designed to turn the Echo into a more capable smart speaker, with better audio quality and the ability to control smart home gadgets.

The Amazon Echo comes in a range of colours, and you can customise them.

The Amazon Echo Show is designed to replace the screen on an old-style Echo with a touchscreen that you can use to make video calls and watch videos.

Its screen is larger than the Echo, and comes with a built-in speaker and a 5-megapixel camera that can shoot high quality video.

Echo Plus

The Echo Plus is a version of the Echo which has better audio quality and has a built-in smart hub that allows you to control smart home gadgets with your voice.

The Echo Plus is also available in charcoal and sandstone colours, and has better audio quality.

The Amazon Echo Plus is available for pre-order starting today.

Amazon Video

Amazon Video will allow you to access Amazon's streaming video service without having to purchase another Amazon Prime subscription

Amazon Video will allow you to access Amazon's streaming video service without having to purchase another Amazon Prime subscription.

The new Echo Connect

The Echo Connect connects to a phone line to make hands-free calls

The Echo Connect is a speakerphone designed for hooking up to a landline phone.

The Echo Connect will be available for pre-order starting today.

Amazon is launching Echo Show and Echo Spot

Amazon has announced the Echo Show, a speaker with a screen, as well as Echo Spot, an alarm clock with a display.

Echo Show and Echo Spot work with a new feature called 'Drop In'.

This allows the Echo devices to automatically connect to other Echo devices around the house, so that, for example, a parent can ask their kid if they want to tell them about a video they saw on YouTube.

Echo Show is available for pre-order starting today, and is set to launch on October 11.

The Amazon Echo Show will be available for pre-order starting today.

The Echo Input is a low-cost Echo with built-in microphones that connects to a receiver, so you can use it as a sound bar

Amazon is releasing a speaker with a built-in microphone

that connects to a receiver, so you can use it as a sound bar.

The Echo Input is available for pre-order starting today, and is set to launch on October 11.

Amazon is also releasing a new smart home security camera called Cloud Cam, which is priced at $119.99 and will be available from today

The Amazon Cloud Cam is a connected security camera that can stream footage to your smartphone

Cloud Cam will cost $119.99 and will be available from today.

It will allow customers to manage their smart home with a smartphone app.

Amazon is also releasing an Amazon Smart Plug, which is a $25 device that lets you control any light or appliance with Alexa.

The smart plug will be available to buy from today, and can be pre-ordered on Amazon today.

Amazon is launching a second-generation Echo, which costs $99.99 and is available for pre-order starting today.

The Echo will get new features including hands-free calling, and Amazon will release a new Echo Plus that costs $149.99

Echo also gains features including hands-free calling and improved stereo pairing.

Amazon will also release the new Echo Look, which is a smart camera that allows customers to take full-length photos and video of their outfits

The Echo Look is an internet-connected camera that takes full-length photos and video of your outfits

The device uses a depth-sensing camera to automatically generate several photos of your outfit, then recommends items you may want to buy.

It will cost $199.99 and is available for pre-order starting today.

Amazon is releasing a second-generation Echo, which costs $99.99 and is available for pre-order starting today.

The device gets new features including hands-free calling and improved stereo pairing.

It will also get a speed boost, and will be 30 percent faster in everything except music playback, Amazon said.

An Amazon Smart Plug (left) and an Amazon Cloud Cam (right) will also be released in the US today

Amazon is also releasing a new smart home security camera called Cloud Cam, which costs $119.

Cloud Cam can stream footage to your smartphone or work as a home alarm, and also allows customers to check in on their homes remotely.

Amazon is also releasing the new Echo Look, which is a camera that can take full-length photos and video of your outfits.

Amazon said the camera will allow customers to shop for new clothes via Amazon Echo Look.

Users will be able to take photos and videos of their outfits, and have the Echo Look advise them on how to dress.

Amazon also released a new smart plug, which is a $25 device that lets customers control any light or appliance with Alexa.

The device will allow customers to automate lights or plugs with a smartphone app, and will cost $24.99.

The gadget is available to pre-order today and will be released on October 11.

Amazon is launching a new second-generation Echo, which costs $99.99 and is available for pre-order starting today.

The Echo (left) will get new features including hands-free calling and improved stereo pairing. The Echo Plus (right) will cost $149.99

The Echo Plus will cost $149.99 and will be available for pre-order starting today.

It will get a speed boost, and will be 30 percent faster in everything except music playback, Amazon said.

The Echo Plus can also control smart home devices, such as lights or thermostats.

The new Amazon Smart Plug costs $24.99 and will be available for pre-order today.

The Amazon Cloud Cam will also be launched today, and is currently available to buy on the Amazon website.

It is unclear when the Cloud Cam will be available in stores.

Amazon Echo Show will also be launched today, but there is no price available yet.

It will be available to pre-order on the Amazon website today and will be released on October 11.

The device is meant to be a digital assistant that can screen your video calls with the front-facing camera, and will be $229.99.

Amazon Echo Show will also be launched today, but there is no price available yet. It is meant to be a digital assistant that can screen your video calls with the front-facing camera

Amazon announced it will release a new Alexa device aimed at controlling smart home gadgets, as well as an all-new Amazon Smart Plug.

The new device will include all of the same features as Echo Show, but will be specifically designed to control smart home products and be used with voice commands, rather than just in the web browser.

The new smart plug will also come with an LED light ring and a physical mute button.

Both devices are available for pre-order today and will be released on October 11.

Echo Show comes with a 7-inch touchscreen display and supports far-field voice recognition, allowing it to hear and respond to voice commands from across the room.

The new Amazon Cloud Cam costs $119.99 and will be available for pre-order today.

The new Amazon Smart Plug costs $24.99 and will be available for pre-order today. It is unclear when the Cloud Cam will be available in stores.

Conclusion

How to start using Amazon Echo?

Amazon Echo can be your best friend if you're interested in smart home devices. It can help you set up and manage the various smart gadgets by connecting them to your smartphone, your office's Wi-Fi or Amazon's network.

You can speak commands to your Echo and it will respond, and then you can access the various functions that the device offers.

While you can tell Alexa to dim the lights, set the temperature in your home or even activate your favourite music and play it on a Spotify playlist, if you don't know what you want to do just speak, Alexa will offer you relevant options.

How to use Amazon Echo?

Launch the Alexa App on your Android or iOS phone and tap the menu button in the top left corner > device settings. Scroll down and tap the microphone icon at the top right corner. Navigate to the Alexa App > My Devices, select your Amazon Echo, and you can set the Echo up from there.

It's important that you connect your Echo to your home Wi-Fi or Amazon's network.

The first step to setting up your Echo is to make sure it's compatible with your Wi-Fi. Do this by looking up the Wi-Fi password for your router. Next, open the Alexa App on your phone and tap the menu button in the top left corner > device settings. Scroll down and tap the mic icon at the top right corner. Navigate to the Alexa App > My Devices, select your Amazon Echo, and you can set the Echo up from there.

Up next, it's a matter of connecting the Echo to your home Wi-Fi or Amazon's network. To do this, you will need to open your router's Wi-Fi settings. Open the settings on your phone and navigate to the network you'd like your Echo to connect to. Tap the SSID (Service Set Identifier) and SSID password, then enter them into the field. Follow the prompts to connect to the network.

Open your router's settings again. Navigate to the top right of the router and select Settings > Network & Internet > Advanced > Check if Network is Networks.

If your Wi-Fi has a password, then you can press the CTRL+V or select Reset. If it doesn't have a password, then you will need to enter the WEP or WPA password for the network. Press the CTRL+V or select Reset.

Now you are connected to your home Wi-Fi. Open the Alexa App on your phone and tap the menu button in the top left corner > device settings. Scroll down and tap the microphone icon at the top right corner. Navigate to the Alexa App > My Devices, select your Amazon Echo, and you can set the Echo up from there.

In order to set up the Amazon Echo, you first have to connect your smartphone or tablet to the Amazon Alexa app. In this step, you need to open the app and log into your Amazon account, if you haven't already. It will prompt you to link your Amazon Echo to your account.

Navigate to the Setting tab, and on the left-hand side, tap the link for the Devices option. Click 'Add'. A screen will appear, with a row of all of your connected devices along the bottom. From the left-hand side, choose your Amazon Echo, tap Add Device.

Finally, choose Alexa, then follow the steps to set up your Echo.

Once the process is complete, you will be asked to enter your Wi-Fi password. If you don't have an Amazon Echo or Amazon account, then you will need to create one. If you want to set up Alexa on multiple devices, tap the plus icon and you can add as many devices as you like. Finally, set up Alexa as your default speaker.

How to use Amazon Echo every day?

Here's how to ask Alexa about the weather and more

Echo devices are designed to help you get quick answers or just add a skill to your routine.

Here are some of the ways you can get your Amazon Echo device up and running in minutes, from getting weather updates to asking for the latest tech news.

One of the first things you need to set up an Amazon Echo or other Alexa device is an account. You can link a variety of services and apps to your Amazon account or you can set up a new one. Either way, just follow these steps to get started:

The Alexa app: Tap the menu button on the left of the screen and then select Settings. From there, choose Sign in to Amazon or the Sign in to Amazon Services screen.

Choose the Amazon account you want to use for Alexa. To set up an Amazon account, go to amazon.com/alexa/setup and sign up.

This screen will prompt you to answer questions such as your name, address, and payment information. Once you are connected to your account, you can add more devices and services.

Next, click on the device that you want to set up. On some devices, you can view your Alexa favorites so you can quickly connect to your preferred local radio station or news outlet.

If your Echo device is not connected to your existing home Wi-Fi network, follow these steps to set it up:

The Alexa app: Click the menu button on the left of the screen and then select Settings. From there, choose Connect to Wi-Fi and then select the device you want to connect to your home network. Select the 'On' button and the device will connect to the Wi-Fi.

Amazon Alexa: Click the menu button on the left of the screen and then select Connections. From there, select Home Wi-Fi (if you have more than one Echo device, select each device). Select the device you want to set up and choose the 'On' button. If the device is not connected, choose the 'On' button. Wait for the device to connect and then click on the button to connect. Once the device connects, it will show up in the list of available Alexa devices. If your Echo device is not connected to your home Wi-Fi, follow these steps to set it up:

Open the Alexa app and select the devices icon. Select your Echo device from the list and then click on 'Enable' at the top of the screen. Click on 'Manage Your Bluetooth' and follow the instructions to connect the device to your home Wi-Fi. Once you are connected to the Wi-Fi, go back and select your Alexa device. Click on the button that says 'Connect to Wi-Fi.'

Find Alexa's best features

Alexa has a lot of cool features. You can ask her for the

weather, play music, set timers, control smart home devices, add things to your shopping list, or check your Amazon order history.

Here are the top ways to get the most out of Alexa, according to Amazon:

Making quick searches. Alexa is more powerful than you might think. She can search for information in the thousands of items that are compatible with your Echo. That includes the books on your Kindle, your podcast subscriptions, and the songs in your Spotify library. In most cases, you'll have to ask to add something to your shopping list or your Amazon or Spotify lists.

Alexa is more powerful than you might think. She can search for information in the thousands of items that are compatible with your Echo. That includes the books on your Kindle, your podcast subscriptions, and the songs in your Spotify library. In most cases, you'll have to ask to add something to your shopping list or your Amazon or Spotify lists. Setting timers. You can use Alexa as a timer by saying, "Alexa, set a timer for one hour." Or, you can tell Alexa, "Set a timer for 10 minutes." Then, you can set another timer for the second timer. Just remember to push the little button on the Echo first.

You can use Alexa as a timer by saying, "Alexa, set a timer for one hour." Or, you can tell Alexa, "Set a timer for 10 minutes." Then, you can set another timer for the second timer. Just remember to push the little button on the Echo first. Talking to the Echo in a group setting. In addition to setting timers and searching for answers, you can ask Alexa to play songs, read audiobooks, or tell jokes to a group of people. You'll need to call out her name before asking for anything.

In addition to setting timers and searching for answers, you can ask Alexa to play songs, read audiobooks, or tell jokes to a group of people. You'll need to call out her name before asking for anything. Getting Alexa to read you a story. You can get a free book to read to Alexa by signing up for a book-reading program on Audible. Or, you can ask Alexa to read a section of a book that you've already bought.

You can get a free book to read to Alexa by signing up for a book-reading program on Audible. Or, you can ask Alexa to read a section of a book that you've already bought. Performing music requests. Alexa will play music from your Amazon Prime account.

Alexa will play music from your Amazon Prime account. Adding skills. Alexa has a whole slew of skills that give you control of smart home devices, the weather, and everything else that comes with Amazon. Just say, "Alexa, enable Hotels," to see if any services you use are available through Alexa.

Alexa has a whole slew of skills that give you control of smart home devices, the weather, and everything else that comes with Amazon. Just say, "Alexa, enable Hotels," to see if any services you use are available through Alexa. Sending text messages. You can make free phone calls to other Echo users with Alexa Calling, but you can't send messages.

You can make free phone calls to other Echo users with Alexa Calling, but you can't send messages. Adding reminders. If you're the type of person who forgets things, you can use Alexa to add an alarm to your Echo for things like getting to work or making a doctor's appointment.

If you're the type of person who forgets things, you can use

Alexa to add an alarm to your Echo for things like getting to work or making a doctor's appointment. Making phone calls. You can use Alexa to call any landline or mobile phone number in the U.S. or Canada.

You can use Alexa to call any landline or mobile phone number in the U.S. or Canada. Finding and playing songs. You can tell Alexa to play a specific song from a songbook you have on your Echo, or you can ask her to play a general category of songs.

You can tell Alexa to play a specific song from a songbook you have on your Echo, or you can ask her to play a general category of songs. Sending a text message. You can use Alexa to send a text message from a third-party app. Just ask her to text you a message. She can even find your contact information from your address book.

You can use Alexa to send a text message from a third-party app. Just ask her to text you a message. She can even find your contact information from your address book. Sending money. You can use Alexa to transfer money from your bank account to your Amazon account. Just say, "Alexa, send Bobby $10."

You can use Alexa to transfer money from your bank account to your Amazon account. Just say, "Alexa, send Bobby $10." Discovering local businesses. There are thousands of skills that allow you to find local restaurants, bars, and bookstores. You can also ask Alexa to play a local comedy or radio show on Pandora or TuneIn.

There are thousands of skills that allow you to find local restaurants, bars, and bookstores. You can also ask Alexa to play a local comedy or radio show on Pandora or TuneIn. Scheduling appointments. Alexa can help you to keep track of your upcoming calendar events and appointments. She can make phone calls, set recurring appointments, set reminders, and even call in sick for you.

In short, Alexa isn't the one-stop device that she has been made out to be. Still, it's nice to know that with Amazon Prime, you can get a device that you can use to control everything from your house to your car and almost anywhere you go. The feature list alone is worth a few bucks a month.

What to know before using Alexa?

You need to know a few things before connecting your phone and Echo devices. Make sure you have the latest version of the Alexa app on your phone.

On the latest app update, you will be able to use Alexa with your phone to make calls. For more on how to do this, check here. You need the latest version of the Alexa app in order to do this.

Make sure Alexa is connected to your account.

Your Alexa devices, whether connected to your home network or through your phone, must be connected to your Amazon account.

Echo can only contact contacts that are in your contacts list. You can create new contacts and call them from Alexa. Make sure your contacts are up to date.

You can ask Alexa to call anyone on your contact list by simply saying "Alexa, call [contact name]".

Alexa will call the person on the contact list by default. You can change this by saying "Alexa, call [contact name] from my contacts."

If your contact doesn't answer or declines to answer, Alexa will say, "I'm sorry, I did not get a response from [contact name]". To prevent your Echo from calling the wrong person, you can say "Alexa, stop calling [contact name]" or "Alexa, stop calling [contact name]".

If you don't like Alexa calling you, there are some things you can do. To change the default contact to someone else, you can say "Alexa, stop calling [contact name]". You can also change the default by opening the Alexa app and going to "Settings".

You can also disable calls altogether in Settings. Click "Accounts" and then click "Calling and messaging". From here you can select either "Enabled" or "Disabled".

Your Echo can also call another Echo. To do this, you need to turn off the ability for other Echos to call you. To do this, say "Alexa, turn off calling other Echos".

Alexa also has a "Calendar" section in the Alexa app. Click the calendar icon and then click the little calendar that says "Calls" or the little calendar that says "Video calls".

If your calendar has a "Calls" or "Video calls" field, it is the field that is called "Call".

To enable video calling with your Alexa devices, open the Alexa app and click on the Calendar icon.

Then click the little calendar icon that says "Video calls" or the little calendar that says "Calls".

Click "Video Calling". To disable video calling, go to the "Calls" section and click "Video Calling".

Finally, if you need help getting your Echo to call a contact, or if you are new to using Alexa, check out our guide on how to get started with Alexa.

Take a look at our list of the best Alexa speakers to help you decide which Echo to buy.

Alexa-enabled Amazon devices

Amazon has announced a number of new Alexa devices. Here are the devices that have been announced or are due to launch this year.

Echo Show

The second generation Echo Show (pictured above) is the successor to the original Echo Show. The device has a 7-inch touchscreen, which can show music videos, tell you the news and even show you your calendar. You can also make video calls through the device.

The Echo Show has a built-in video camera so that you can make video calls to anyone who also has an Echo Show. Amazon has added a second, front-facing camera to enable video calling for the first time.

Echo Spot

The Echo Spot (pictured below) is an Alexa-enabled device that is meant to be an alternative to the Echo Dot. The Spot comes with a circular screen on top and can show you video clips, play music and read the news.

Echo Buttons

The Echo Buttons (pictured below) are another new Amazon product, but rather than doing anything other than playing games, they can also be used to interact with Alexa. You can use them to play "Skills", or Alexa's own software, games that have been created by third-party developers. They cost $19.99 each (£15).

Echo Buttons can also be connected to an Echo Dot to enable interactive responses and a game of Pong.

Echo Input

The Echo Input (pictured below) is a way to turn any speaker into an Alexa-enabled speaker. Using Wi-Fi, Bluetooth or a 3.5mm audio cable, you can add Alexa into any speaker and use it as your personal assistant. The Echo Input costs $39.99 (£34.99).

Echo Auto

Amazon has also launched an Alexa-enabled device for drivers. The Echo Auto, which is designed to be a dash-mounted Alexa device, has 360-degree microphones that can pick up your voice commands from any direction. Amazon's announcement claims that it can hear you from around 20 feet away, even when music is playing.

Amazon Dash Button

The Amazon Dash Button is a new way to order something from Amazon using only your voice. When you press the button, you can order an item from Amazon that is already on its way to you. Amazon says that you can use it to order: household essentials, pet supplies and select baby products.

Amazon Spark

Amazon has launched Spark, which is a social network that the company says is designed to let you talk to your friends and share pictures and videos. To use Spark, all you need to do is ask Alexa to "Spark me". Alexa will then ask you for a picture or a video that you want to share.

Amazon will automatically pair you with other Spark users in your area who are also using the app. There is also a new "Follow Me" feature, which means that you can follow other Spark users who live close to you and you'll see their activity stream.

Amazon Echo Input

Amazon Echo Input (pictured below) is an Alexa device that is designed to allow someone to build a speaker using a range of smart home hubs. With the Input, you can plug it into a speaker and have Alexa built into the speaker.

It is designed to allow someone to "control the music by tapping or saying the name of the song, artist, or playlist you're listening to" , says Amazon.

Amazon Dash Wand

The Amazon Dash Wand is a new Alexa device that enables you to use Alexa to order products from Amazon without having to use the Alexa app. Amazon says that "weeks of training" will be required, but that all you need to do is wave the wand at the product and it will be added to your shopping list.

Amazon Tap

The Amazon Tap is a portable Alexa device that is designed to be used while you are on the move. With the Tap, you can ask Alexa to play music or read the news, and you can do the same by tapping the microphone button or pressing the on-screen menu button.

Amazon Echo Plus

The Echo Plus is a smart home hub that can control smart home products. Amazon says that it has many smart home features including "mass-micromanage your smart home", "assign timers and settings to any device", and "keep track of your daily routines by setting timers for lights, thermostats, and more".

Amazon Echo Plus + Philips Hue Bulb

The Echo Plus + Philips Hue Bulb is a smart home hub that allows you to use Alexa to control your Philips Hue light bulbs. You can use the Amazon Echo Plus as a hub so that you can easily control Hue lights from your Echo devices and your Echo Plus. The Echo Plus has many smart home features including "assign tasks to your Hue lights", "use voice to control your Hue lights, schedule light cycles", and "control your lights by group".

Amazon Echo Show

The Echo Show is a new Echo device that has a 7-inch touchscreen that is designed to display news, weather, and videos. The device also has a camera that allows you to make video calls, and it is always listening for the wake word "Alexa".

The Echo Show has many smart home features including

"use your camera to see and talk to the room you're in", "make video calls to anyone with a Echo Show or the Alexa app", and "listen for the Echo Show to answer your questions and show you information while you're on the go".

Amazon Echo Spot

The Echo Spot is a new Echo device with a round display that offers a visual element to Alexa's responses. The Echo Spot is designed to display Alexa's responses on the screen while Alexa keeps listening.

Amazon Smart Plug

The Amazon Smart Plug is a Wi-Fi smart plug that allows you to turn your regular light or appliance on or off from a voice command or via the Alexa app.

Amazon Smart Bulb

The Amazon Smart Bulb is a smart bulb that is designed to be used with an Amazon Echo. It allows you to set lighting scenes, and you can ask Alexa to set the colour of the lights, change the mood of the room, and control the brightness.

Amazon Cloud Cam

The Amazon Cloud Cam is a security camera designed to let you see and monitor your home without using a traditional home security system. You can use the Cloud Cam to see and hear what's happening in your home and you can control it remotely.

Amazon Cloud Cam + Echo Dot

The Amazon Cloud Cam + Echo Dot is a smart home camera bundle that allows you to see and hear what's happening in your home while you're away and it has a built-in smart speaker that allows you to use Alexa to control your home. You can ask Alexa to send a doorbell alert or show the security camera's live feed on your Echo Dot.

Amazon Fire TV Cube

The Amazon Fire TV Cube is an Alexa-powered streaming device that you can use to watch movies, TV shows, and more. The Fire TV Cube also allows you to use your voice to control your media. You can control any HDMI-enabled device by using your voice, and you can use it to turn your TV on or off or to change channels, and you can control it from anywhere in the house with your voice. You can also use Alexa to play games on your TV.

Amazon Kindle Paperwhite

The Kindle Paperwhite is an ebook reader designed to offer a large, high-resolution display for reading books and magazines. It is waterproof and has a built-in light for reading in the dark.

You can charge the Kindle Paperwhite using the included charging cable, which you can also use to charge your other gadgets, or with a USB cable that you can buy separately for $20 (£14.99).

Amazon Kindle Oasis

The Amazon Kindle Oasis is an ebook reader designed to offer a large, high-resolution display for reading books and magazines. It is waterproof and has a built-in light for reading in the dark.

You can charge the Kindle Oasis using the included charging cable, which you can also use to charge your other gadgets, or with a USB cable that you can buy separately for $20 (£14.99).

What advantages of Amazon Echo devices?

Amazon Echo devices are better than home assistant appliances due to its highly user-friendly. Some of the advantages of these devices are:

They help in hands-free interaction between you and other devices like it recognizes your voice over WiFi and it is not connected to your home network. It also understands more than ten different voices.

You can connect Amazon Echo devices with your TV, which is really helpful, as you can use these devices to answer all the questions or find the answer to your queries or perform other actions through your TV.

Amazon Echo devices don't come with any external speaker and these are supposed to work through a Wi-Fi connected speaker, which means it doesn't have any potential to connect with other devices like TVs, computer speakers etc.

They are more useful with the help of third-party app integration features, which helps in accomplishing the tasks.

How to integrate a home assistant appliance with your Amazon Echo device?

There is no specific way to integrate the devices. You can do it via the software updates and user-friendly app.

You can use Alexa App to connect your Echo devices to

your smartphone or computer.

The basic concept is to follow the steps below to do the integration process.

Go to Alexa App on your device or computer.

Tap on the icon and tap on Settings.

Tap on "Link my Devices"

You should choose your home assistant appliance.

You should be connected to a Wi-Fi network.

Scroll down and select "Add Device."

Select your home assistant appliance.

If you don't have that particular appliance, then you can use a device you already have.

Once you select your device, you need to sign in to your Amazon account.

You can also change your default Amazon Echo device by following the same steps.

The home assistant appliance will be a few seconds behind to recognize your voice. It is an Alexa device by default.

It is advisable to configure Alexa in such a way that your device is ready to hear the wake word "Alexa".

Enable "Alexa on OFF" setting. This will ensure that you don't have to listen to the voice request.

Printed in Great Britain
by Amazon

72160424R00122